SOME EMINENT WOMEN OF OUR TIMES · VOLU GARRETT FAWCETT (DAME)

Publisher's Note

The book descriptions we ask book-sellers to display prominently warn that this is an historic book with numerous typos, missing text or index and is not illustrated.

We scanned this book using character recognition software that includes an automated spell check. Our software is 99 percent accurate if the book is in good condition. However, we do understand that even one percent can be a very annoying number of typos! And sometimes all or part of a page is missing from our copy of a book. Or the paper may be so discolored from age that you can no longer read the type. Please accept our sincere apologies.

After we re-typeset and design a book, the page numbers change so the old index and table of contents no longer work. Therefore, we usually remove them.

Our books sell so few copies that you would have to pay hundreds of dollars to cover the cost of proof reading and fixing the typos, missing text and index. Therefore, whenever possible, we let our customers download a free copy of the original typo-free scanned book. Simply enter the barcode number from the back cover of the paperback in the Free Book form at www.general-books.net. You may also qualify for a free trial membership in our book club to download up to four books for free. Simply enter the barcode number from the back cover onto the membership form on the same page. The book club entitles you to select from more than a million books at no additional charge. Simply enter the title or subject onto the search form to find the books.

If you have any questions, could you please be so kind as to consult our Frequently Asked Questions page at www.general-books.net/faqs.cfm? You are also welcome to contact us there.

General Books LLC™, Memphis, USA, 2012. ISBN: 9781154422962.

❧ ❧ ❧ ❧ ❧ ❧ ❧ ❧

ELIZABETH FRY

"Humanity is erroneously considered among the commonplace virtues. If it deserved such a place there would be less urgent need than, alas! there is for its daily exercise among us. In its pale shape of kindly sentiment and bland pity it is common enough, and is always the portion of the cultivated. But humanity armed, aggressive, and alert, never slumbering and never wearying, moving like an ancient hero over the land to slay monsters, is the rarest of virtues."—John Morley.

The present century is one that is distinguished by the active part women have taken in careers that were previously closed to them. Some people would have us believe that if women write books, paint pictures, and understand science and ancient languages, they will cease to be true women, and cease to care for those womanly occupations and responsibilities that have always been entrusted to them. This is an essentially false and mistaken notion. True cultivation of the understanding makes a sensible woman value at their real high worth all her womanly duties, and so far from making her neglect them, causes her to appreciate them more highly than she would otherwise have dona It has always been held—at least, in Christian countries—that the most womanly of women's duties are to be found in works of mercy to those who are desolate and miserable. To be thirsty, hungry, naked, sick, or in prison, is to have a S B claim for compassion and comfort upon womanly pity and tenderness. And we shall see, if we look back over recent years, that never have these womanly tasks been more zealously fulfilled than they have been in the century which has produced Elizabeth Fry, Florence Nightingale, Josephine Butler, and Octavia Hill.

Mrs. Fry was born before the begin-ning of this century —in 1780—but the great public work with which her memory will always be connected was not begun till about 1813. She was born of the wealthy Quaker family, the Gurneys of Norwich. Her parents were not very strict members of the sect to which they belonged, for they allowed their children to learn music and dancing—pursuits that were then considered very worldly even by many who did not belong to the Society of Friends. The gentle poet, William Cowper, speaks in one of his letters, written about the time of. Elizabeth Fry's childhood, of love of music as a thing which tends "to weaken and destroy the spiritual discernment." Mr. and Mrs. Gurney, however, seem to have been very free from such prejudices, as well as from others which were much more universal, for their children not only learnt music and dancing, but also—girls as well as boys—Latin and mathematics.

Mrs. Gurney seems to have discerned that she had an especial treasure in her little Elizabeth. She is spoken of in her mother's journal as "my dove-like Betsy." The authoress of the biography of Elizabeth Fry in the Eminent Women series, says: "Her faculty for independent investigation, her unswerving loyalty to duty, and her fearless perseverance in works of benevolence, were all foreshadowed" in her childhood. She had as a young girl what appears to us now a very extraordinary dread of enthusiasm in religion. One would think that if ever a woman needed enthusiasm for her life's work, Elizabeth Fry was that woman. But she confesses in her journal, written when she was seventeen years of age, " the greatest fear of religion" because it is generally allied with enthusiasm. Perhaps the truth is that she had so deep a natural fount of enthusiasm in her heart that she dreaded the work that it would impel her to, when once it was allowed a free course. She had a very strong, innate repugnance to anything which drew public attention upon herself, and only the imperative sense of duty enabled her to overcome this feeling. In her heart she said what her Master had said before her: "Father, if it be possible, let this cup pass from me."

When the sphere of public duty first revealed itself to her, she records in her diary what it cost her to enter upon it, and writes of it as "the humiliating path that has appeared to be opening before me." It must be noticed, however, that in her case, as always, the steep and difficult path of duty becomes easier to those who do not flinch from it. In a later passage of her diary, the public work which she had at first called a path of humiliation she speaks of as "this great mercy."

In the little book to which reference has just been made, we read that the first great change in Elizabeth Gurney's life was caused by the deep impression made upon her by the sermons of William Savery. It is rather strange to find the girl who had such a terror of enthusiasm, weeping passionately while William Savery was preaching. Her sister has described what took place. "Betsy astonished us all by the great feeling she showed. She wept most of the way home.... What she went through in her own mind I cannot say; but the results were most powerful and most evident" (p. 11, *Elizabeth Fry.* By Mrs. E. R. Pitman). Her emotion was not of the kind that passes away and leaves no trace behind. The whole course of her life and tenor of her thoughts were changed. She became a strict Quakeress, not, however, without some conflict with herself. There are pleasant little touches of human nature in the facts that she found it a trial to say "thee" and "thou," and to give up her scarlet riding habit. Soon after this, at the age of twenty, she became the wife of Mr. Joseph Fry, and removed to London, where she lived in St. Mildred's Court, in the City. The family into which she married were Quakers, like her own, but of a much more severe and strict kind. Her marriage was, however, in every respect a fortunate one. Her husband sympathised

deeply with her in all her efforts for the good of others, and encouraged her in her public work, although many in the Society of Friends did not scruple to protest that a married woman has no duties except to her husband and children. Her journal shows how anxiously she guarded herself against any temptation to neglect her home duties. She was a tender and devoted mother to her twelve children, and it was through her knowledge of the strength of a mother's love that she was able to reach the hearts of many of the poor prisoners whom she afterwards helped out of the wretchedness into which they had fallen.

Her study of the problem, how to help the poor, began in this way. A beggar-woman with a child in her arms stopped her in the street. Mrs. Fry, seeing that the child had whooping-cough and was dangerously ill, offered to go with the woman to her home in order more effectually to assist her. To Mrs. Fry's surprise, the woman immediately tried to make off; it was evident what she wanted was a gift of money, not any help to the suffering child. Mrs. Fry followed her, and found that her rooms were filled with a crowd of farmed-out children in every stage of sickness and misery; the more pitiable the appearance of one of these poor mites, the more useful an implement was it in the beggar's stock-in-trade. From this time onwards the condition of women and children in the lowest and most degraded of the criminal classes became the study of Mrs. Fry's life. She had the gift of speech on any subject which deeply moved her. From about 1809 she began to speak at the Friends' meeting-house. This power of speaking, as well as working, enabled her to draw about her an active band of co-workers. "When she first began visiting the female prisoners in Newgate it is probable that she could not have supported all that she had to go through if it had not been for the sympathy and companionship of Anna Buxton and other Quaker ladies whom she had roused through her power of speech, just as she had herself been roused when a girl by the preaching of William Savery."

The condition of the women and children in Newgate Prison, when Mrs. Fry first began visiting them in 1813, was more horrible than anything that can be easily imagined. Three hundred poor wretches were herded together in two wards and two cells, with no furniture, no bedding of any kind, and no arrangements for decency or privacy. Cursing and swearing, foul language, and personal filthiness, made the dens in which the women were confined equally offensive to ear, eye, nose, and sense of modesty. The punishment of death at that time existed for 300 different offences, and though there were many mitigations of the sentence in the case of those who had only committed minor breaches of the law, yet the fact that nearly all had by law incurred the penalty of death, gave an apparent justification for herding the prisoners indiscriminately together. It thus happened that many a poor girl who had committed a comparatively trivial offence, became absolutely ruined in body and mind through her contact in prison with the vilest and most degraded of women. No attempt whatever was made to reform or discipline the prisoners, or to teach them any trade whereby, on leaving the gaol, they might earn an honest livelihood. Add to this that there were no female warders nor female officers of any kind in the prison, and that the male warders were frequently men of depraved life, and it is not difficult to see that no element of degradation was wanting to make the female wards of Newgate what they were often called— a hell on earth.

When Elizabeth Fry and Anna Buxton first visited this Inferno, there was so little pretence at any kind of control over the prisoners, that the Governor of Newgate advised the ladies to leave their watches behind them at home. Mrs. Fry, with a wise instinct, felt that the best way of influencing the poor, wild, rough women was to show her care for their children. Many of the prisoners had their children with them in gaol, and there were very few even of the worst who could not be reached by care for their little ones. Even those who had no children were often not without the motherly instinct, and could be roused to some measure of self-restraint and decency for the sake of the children who were being corrupted by their example. So Mrs. Fry's first step towards reforming the women took the form of starting a school for the children in the prison. As usual in all good work of a novel kind, those who knew nothing about it were quite sure that Mrs. Fry would have been much more usefully employed if she had turned her energies in a different direction. People who have never stirred a finger to lighten the misery of mankind always know, so much better than the workers, what to do and how to do it. They would probably tell a fireman who is entering a burning house at the risk of his life, that he would be more usefully employed in studying the chemical action of fire, or in pondering over the indestructibility of matter. The popular feeling with regard to Mrs. Fry's work in Newgate was embodied by Thomas Hood in a ballad which is preserved in his collected works, and serves now to show how wrong a good and tender-hearted man may be in passing judgment on a work of the value of which he was entirely unqualified to form an opinion. The refrain of the poem is "Keep your school out of Newgate, Mrs. Fry "—

I like the pity in your full-brimmed eye.
I like your carriage and your silken gray,
Your dove-like habits and your silent preaching,
But I *don't* like your Newgatory teaching.

No, I'll be your friend, and like a friend
Point out your very worst defect. Nay, never
Start at that word! But I must ask you why
You keep your 3chool in Newgate, Mrs. Fry.

Mrs. Fry's philanthropy was not of a kind to be checked by a ballad, and she went on perseveringly with her work; the school was formed, and a prisoner, named Mary Cormor, was the first schoolmistress. A wonderful change gradually became apparent in the demeanour, language, and appearance of the women in prison. In 1817 an association was formed for carrying on the work Mrs. Fry had begun. It was called "An Association for the Improvement of the Female Prisoners in Newgate." Its first members were eleven Quakeresses and one clergyman's wife. Public attention was now alive to the importance of the work; and in the following year a Select Committee of the House of Commons was appointed to inquire and report upon the condition of the London prisons. Mrs. Fry was examined before this committee. Her chief recommendations were that the prisoners should be employed in some industry, and be paid for their work, and that good conduct should be encouraged by rewards; she was also most urgent that the women prisoners should be in the charge of women warders. Her work in the prison naturally led her to consider the condition and ultimate fate of women who were transported. Transportation was then carried out upon a large scale, and all the evils of the prison existed in an intensified form on board the transport ships. The horrors of the voyage were followed by a brutal and licentious distribution of the women on their arrival to colonists, soldiers, and convicts, who went on board and took their choice of the human cargo. Mrs. Fry's efforts resulted in a check being placed on these shameful barbarities. The women were, owing to her exertions, sent out in charge of female warders, and they were provided with decent accommodation on their arrival.

Like Howard, Mrs. Fry did not confine her efforts to the poor and wretched of her own country. She visited foreign countries in order thoroughly to study various methods of prison work and discipline. On one occasion she found in Paris a congenial task in bringing the force of public opinion to bear on the treatment of children in the Foundling Hospital there. The poor babies were done up in swaddling clothes that were only unwrapped once in twelve hours. There was no healthy screaming in the wards, only a sound that a hearer compared to the faint and pitiful bleating of lambs. A lady who visited the hospital said she never made the round of the spotlessly clean white cots, without finding at least one dead baby! Everything in the hospital was regulated by clockwork; its outward appearance was clean and orderly in the extreme, but the babies died like flies! The Archbishop of Paris was vastly annoyed with Mrs. Fry for pointing out this drawback to the perfect organisation of the institution; but when once the light was let in, improvement followed.

There were many other classes of neglected or unfortunate people whose circumstances were improved by Mrs. Fry's exertions. The lonely shepherds of Salisbury Plain were provided with a library after she had visited the desolate region where they lived. She also organised a lending library for coastguardsmen and for domestic servants. There was no end to her active exertions for the good of others except that of her life.

She died at Ramsgate in 1845, and was buried at Barking.

Her private life was not without deep sorrows and anxieties. She lost a passionately beloved child in 1815; in 1828 her husband was unfortunate in his business affairs. They suffered from a great diminution of fortune, and were obliged to remove to a smaller house and adopt a less expensive style of living. She did not pretend to any indifference she was far from feeling under these trials; but they were powerless to turn her from the duties which she had marked out for herself. The work which she had undertaken for the good of others probably became, in its turn, her own solace and support in the hour of trial and affliction. In helping others she had unconsciously built up a strong refuge for herself, thus giving a new illustration to the truth of the words: "He that findeth his life shall lose it: and he that loseth his life, for my sake, shall find it." II MARY CARPENTER

"That it may please Thee... to show Thy pity upon all prisoners and captives."

Mary Carpenter was

years old when Mrs. Fry died in 1845. We do not hear, in reading the lives of either, that the two women ever met, or that the elder directly stimulated the activity of the younger. Yet the one most surely prepared the way for the other; their work was upon the same lines, and Miss Carpenter, the Unitarian, of Bristol, was the spiritual heir and successor of Mrs. Fry, the Quaker, of Norwich.

There is, it is true, a contrast in the manner in which the two women approached their work in life. The aim of both was the rescue of what Mary Carpenter called "the perishing and dangerous classes." But while Mrs. Fry was led, through her efforts on behalf of convicts, to establish schools for them and their children, Mary Carpenter's first object was the school for neglected children, and through the knowledge gained there she was led to form schemes for the reformation of criminals and for a new system of prison discipline. Mrs. Fry worked through convicts to schools; Mary Carpenter through schools to convicts.

It will not therefore be imagined that there is any want of appreciation of Mrs. Fry when it is said that Mary Carpenter's labours were more effective, inasmuch as they were directed to the cause of the evil, rather than to its results. By establishing reformatory and industrial schools, and by obtaining, after long years of patient effort, the sanction and support of Parliament for them, she virtually did more than had up to that time ever been done in England, to stop the supply of criminals. Children who were on the brink of crime, and those who had actually fallen into criminal courses, were, through her efforts, snatched away from their evil surroundings, and helped to become respectable and industrious men and women. Before her time, magistrates and judges had no choice, when a child criminal stood convicted before them, but to sentence him to prison, whence he would probably come out hopelessly corrupted and condemned for life to the existence of a beast of prey. She says, in one of her letters, dated 1850: "A Bristol magistrate told me that for twenty years he

had felt quite unhappy at going on committing these young culprits. And yet he had *done* nothing!" The worse than uselessness of prisons for juvenile offenders was a fact that was burnt into Mary Carpenter's mind and heart by the experience of her life. She was absolutely incapable of recognising the evil and at the same time calmly acquiescing in it. Her magisterial friend is the type of the common run of humanity, who satisfy their consciences by saying, "Very grievous! very wrong!" and who do nothing to remove the grievance and the wrong; she is the type of the knights-errant of humanity, who never see a wrong without assailing it, and endeavouring to remove the causes which produce it.

Mary Carpenter was born at Exeter in 1807, the eldest of five children, several of whom have left their mark on the intellectual and moral history of this century. There was all through her life a great deal of the elder sister— one may almost say, of the mother—in Mary Carpenter. In an early letter her mother speaks of the wonderfully tranquillising influence of dolls on her little Mary. She never shrank from responsibility, and she had a special capacity for protecting love—a capacity that stood her in good stead in reclaiming the little waifs and strays to whom she afterwards devoted herself. Her motherliness comes out in a hundred ways in the story of her life. Her endless patience with the truant and naughty children was such as many a real mother might envy. She was especially proud of the title of "the old mother" which the Indian women, whom she visited towards the close of her life, gave her. In writing to a friend, she once said: "There is a verse in the prophecies, 1 have given thee children whom thou hast not borne,' and the motherly love of my heart has been given to many who have never known before a mother's love." She adopted a child in 1858 to be a daughter to her, and writes gleefully: "Just think of me with a little girl of *my own 1* about five years old, readymade to my hand, without the trouble of marrying—a darling little thing, an orphan,"

etc. etc. Her friends spoke of her eager delight in buying the baby's outfit.

It was her motherliness that made her so successful with the children in the reformatories and industrial schools; moreover, the children believed in her love for them. One little ragged urchin told a clergyman that Miss Carpenter was a lady who gave away all her money for naughty boys, and only kept enough to make herself clean and decent. On one occasion she heard that two of her ex-pupils had "got into trouble," and were in prison at Winchester. She quickly found an opportunity of visiting them, and one of them exclaimed, directly he saw her, "Oh! Miss Carpenter, I knew you would not desert us!"

Another secret of her power, and also of her elasticity of spirit, was her sense of humour. It was like a silver thread running through her laborious life, saving her from dulness and despondency. In one of her reports, which has to record the return of a runaway, she said: "He came back resembling the prodigal in everything except his repentance!"

The motto which she especially made her own was *Dum doceo disco—While I teach, I learn.* Her father had a school for boys in Bristol, and Mary and her sister were educated in it. They were among the best of their father's pupils, one of whom, the Rev. James Martineau, has left a record of the great impression Mary's learning made upon him. She was indeed very proficient in many branches of knowledge. Her education included Latin, Greek, mathematics, and natural history; and the exactness which her father and the nature of her studies demanded of her, formed a most invaluable training for her after career. For many years the acquisition of knowledge, for its own sake, was the chief joy of her life; but a time came when it ceased to satisfy her. She was rudely awakened from the delightful dreams of a student's life by a severe visitation of cholera at Bristol in 1832. From this period, and indeed from a special day—that set apart as a fast-day in consequence of the cholera—dates a solemn dedication of herself to the service of her fellow-creatures. She wrote in her journal 31st March 1832, what her resolution was, and concluded: "These things I have written to be a witness against me, if ever I should forget what ought to be the object of all my active exertions in life." These solemn self-dedications are seldom or never spoken of by those who make them. Records of them are found sometimes in journals long after the hand that has written them is cold. But, either written or unwritten, they are probably the rule rather than the exception on the part of those who devote themselves to the good of others. The world has recently learned that this was the case with Lord Shaftesbury. There is a time when the knighterrant consciously enrols himself a member of the noble band of warriors against wrong and oppression, and takes upon himself his baptismal vow—manfully to fight against sin, the world, and the devil, and to continue Christ's faithful soldier and servant to his life's end.

It must be remembered that when Mary Carpenter first began to exert herself for the benefit of neglected children, there were no reformatory or industrial schools, except those which had been established by the voluntary efforts of philanthropists like herself. Aided by a band of fellowworkers and wise advisers, chief of whom were Mr. Matthew Davenport Hill, the Recorder of Birmingham, and his daughters; Dr. Tuckerman, of the U.S.A. Mr. Russell Scott, of Bath; Mr. Sheriff Watson, of Aberdeen; and Lady Byron, Mary Carpenter set to work to establish a voluntary reformatory school at Kingswood, near Bristol. Her principle was that by surrounding children, who would otherwise be criminals, with all the influences of a wholesome home life, there was a better chance than by any other course, of reclaiming these children, and making them useful members of society. To herd children together in large, unhomelike institutions, was always, in Mary Carpenter's view, undesirable; the effect on character is bad; the more perfectly such places are managed, the more nearly do the children in them become part of a huge machine, and the

less are their faculties, as responsible human beings, developed. Over and over again, in books, in addresses, and by the example of the institutions which she managed herself, Mary Carpenter reiterated the lesson that if a child is to be rescued and reformed, he must be placed in a family; and that where it is necessary, for the good of society, to separate children on account of their own viciousness, or that of their parents, from their own homes, the institutions receiving them should be based on the family ideal so far as possible. With this end in view, the children at Kingswood were surrounded by as many home influences as possible. Miss Carpenter at one time thought of living there herself, but this scheme was given up, in deference to her mother's wishes. She was, however, a constant visitor, and a little room, which had once been John Wesley's study, was fitted up as a resting-place for her. On a pane of one of the windows of this room her predecessor had written the words, "God is here." She taught the children herself, and provided them with rabbits, fowls, and pigs, the care of which she felt would exercise a humanising influence upon them. The whole discipline of the place was directed by her; one of her chief difficulties was to get a staff of assistants with sufficient faith in her methods to give them an honest trial. She did not believe in a physical force morality. "We must not attempt," she wrote, "to *break* the will,'but to train it to govern itself wisely; and it must be our great aim to call out the good, which exists even in the most degraded, and make it conquer the bad." After a year's work at Kingswood in this spirit, she writes very hopefully of the improvement already visible in the sixteen boys and thirteen girls in her charge. The boys could be trusted to go into Bristol on messages, and even "thievish girls" could be sent out to shops with money, which they never thought of appropriating.

But although the success of the institution was so gratifying, it had no legal sanction; it had consequently no power to deal with runaways, and the great mass of juvenile delinquents were still

sentenced to prisons, from which they emerged, like the man into whom seven devils entered, in a state far worse than their first. Mary Carpenter's work was not only to prove the success of her methods of dealing with young criminals, but, secondly, to convince the Government that the established system was a bad one, and thirdly, and most difficult of all, to get them to legislate on the subject. A long history of her efforts to obtain satisfactory legislation for children of the perishing and dangerous classes is given in her life, written by her nephew, Mr. J. Estlin Carpenter. It is enough here to say that in the House of Lords, Lord Shaftesbury, and in the House of Commons, Sir Stafford Northcote and Mr. Adderley (afterwards Lord Iddesleigh and Lord Norton), were her chief supporters. Mr. Lowe (now Lord Sherbrooke) was her chief opposer. Liberal as she was, born and bred, as well as by heart's conviction, she confessed with some feeling of shame, that the Tories "are best in *this* work." At last, in 1854, her efforts were crowned with success, and the Royal Assent was given to the Youthful Offenders Bill, which authorised the establishment of reformatory schools, under the sanction of the Home Secretary.

It is a striking proof of the change that has taken place in the sphere and social status of women, that Mary Carpenter, in the first half of her active life, suffered what can be called nothing less than anguish, from any effort which demanded from herself the least departure from absolute privacy. When she began her work of convincing the public and Parliament of the principles which ought to govern the education of juvenile criminals, her nephew writes that to have spoken at a conference in the presence of gentlemen, she would have felt, at that time (1851), as tantamount to unsexing herself. When she was called upon to give evidence before a Select Committee of the House of Commons in 1852, her profound personal timidity made the occasion a painful ordeal to her, which she was only enabled to support by the consciousness of the needs of the children. Surely this excessive timidity arises from morbid self-consciousness, rather than from true womanly modesty. Mary Carpenter was enabled, by increasing absorption in her work, to throw it off, and for her work's sake she became able to speak in public with ease and selfpossession. She frequently spoke and read papers at the Social Science Congresses, and at meetings of the British Association. A letter from her brother Philip describes one of these occasions, at the meeting in 1860 of the British Association at Oxford, when her subject was, "Educational Help from the Government Grant to the Destitute and Neglected Children of Great Britain." *"July—, 1860.* "There was a great gathering of celebrities to hear her. It was in one of the ancient schools or lecture-halls, which was crowded, evidently not by the curious, but by those who really wanted to know what she had to say. She stood up and read in her usual clear voice and expressive enunciation.... It was, I suppose, the first time a woman's voice had read a lecture there before dignitaries of learning and the Church; but as there was not the slightest affectation on the one hand, so on the other hand there was neither a scorn nor an etiquettish politeness; but they all listened to her as they would have listened to Dr. Rae about Franklin, only with the additional feeling (expressed by the President, Mr. Nassau Senior) that it was a matter of heart and duty, as well as head."

As years passed by, her work and responsibilities rapidly increased. It is astonishing to read of the number of institutions, from ragged schools upwards, of which she was practically the head and chief. Her thoroughly practical and business-like methods of work, as well as her obvious self-devotion and earnestness, ensured to her a large share of public confidence and esteem, and although she was a Unitarian, sectarian prejudices did not often thwart her usefulness. Two instances to the contrary must, however, be given. In 1856 the Somersetshire magistrates at the Quarter Sessions at Wells refused to sanction the Girls' Reformatory, established by Miss Carpenter at the Red Lodge, Bris-

tol, on account of the religious opinions of its foundress. They appeared to have forgotten that "Pure religion and undefiled before God and the Father is this, to visit the fatherless and widows in their affliction, and to keep himself unspotted from the world." A more deeply and truly religious spirit than Mary Carpenter's never existed; but that is the last thing that sectarian rancour takes heed of. The other little bit of persecution she met with was regarded by herself and her friends as something between a compliment and a joke. In 1864 she wrote a book entitled *Our Convicts.* The work was received with commendation by jurists in France, Germany, and the United States, but the crowning honour of all was that the Pope placed her and her books on the "Index Expurgatorius." After this she felt that if she had lived in earlier times she might have aspired to the crown of martyrdom.

The extraordinary energy and vitality of Mary Carpenter never declined. When she was over sixty years of age she made four successive visits to India, with the double object of arousing public opinion there about the education of women, and the condition of convicts, especially of female convicts. At the age of sixty-six she visited America. She had long been deeply interested in the social and political condition of the United States, and had many warm personal friends there. Her first impulse to reformatory work had come from an American citizen, Dr. Tuckerman; her sympathy and help had been abundantly bestowed upon the Abolitionist party, and she was of course deeply thankful when the Civil War in America ended as it did in the victory of the North, and in the complete abolition of negro slavery in the United States. Her mind remained vigorous and susceptible to new impressions and new enthusiasms to the last. Every movement for elevating the position of women had her encouragement. She frequently showed her approval of the movement for women's suffrage by signing petitions in its favour, and was convinced that legislation affecting both sexes would never

be what it ought to be until women as well as men had the power of voting for Members of Parliament. In 1877, within a month of her death, she signed the memorial to the Senate of the London University in favour of the admission of women to medical degrees.

She passed away peacefully in her sleep, without previous illness or decline of mental powers, in June 1877, leaving an honoured name, and a network of institutions for the reform of young criminals, and the prevention of crime, of which our country will for many years to come reap the benefit.
o "As when by night the glass Of Galileo less assured observes Imagined lands and regions in the moon."—*Paradise Lost.*

Every one knows the fame of Sir William Herschel, the first distinguished astronomer of that name, the builder and designer of the forty-foot telescope, and the discoverer of the planet, called after George III., Georgium Sidus. Hardly less well known is the name of his sister, Caroline Hers.chel, who was her brother's constant helper for fifty years. She was the discoverer of eight comets; she received, for her distinguished services to science, the gold medal of the Royal Astronomical Society, and the gold medal conferred annually by the King of Prussia for science; she was also made an honorary member of the Royal Astronomical Society and of the Royal Irish Academy, and received many other public marks of appreciation of the value of her astronomical labours. Few women have done as much as she for the promotion of science, and few have been more genuinely humble in their estimate of their own attainments. Nothing made her more angry than any praise which appeared, even in the slightest degree, to detract from the reputation of her brother; over and over again she asserted that she was nothing more than a tool which he had taken the trouble to sharpen. One of her favourite expressions about herself was that she only "minded the heavens" for her brother. "I am nothing," she wrote; "I have done nothing: all I am, all I know, I owe to my brother. I am only a tool which he shaped to his use—a well-trained puppy-dog would have done as much."

Scientific men and scientific societies did not endorse Caroline Herschel's extremely humble estimate of herself. In the address to the Astronomical Society by Mr. South, on presenting the medal to Miss Herschel in 1828, the highest praise was conferred upon her as her brother's fellow-worker, and as an original observer. "She it was," said Mr. South, "who reduced every observation, made every calculation; she it was who arranged everything in systematic order; and she it was who helped him (Sir W. Herschel) to obtain his imperishable name. But her claims to our gratitude do not end here: as an original observer she demands, and I am sure she has, our unfeigned thanks." He then narrates the series of her astronomical discoveries, and adds, referring to the brother and sister: "Indeed, in looking at the joint labours of these extraordinary personages, we scarcely know whether most to admire the intellectual power of the brother, or the unconquerable industry of his sister. "

The sharpest tool, or the best-trained puppy-dog in the world, could hardly have earned such praise as this. Without endorsing what Caroline said of herself in her generous wish to heighten the fame of her brother, it must, however, be conceded that in a remarkable degree she was what he made her. With an excellent, and indeed an exceptionally powerful, natural understanding, she was ready to apply it in any direction her brother chose. She was far from being a mere tool, but her mind resembled a fine musical instrument upon which her brother was able to play the lightest air or the grandest symphony, according as he pleased. At his bidding she became, first, a prima donna, then an astronomer; if he had so wished it, she would probably with equal readiness and versatility have turned her attention to any other branch of science or art. Caroline Herschel was, indeed, a fine example of what devoted love can do to elevate the character and develop the natural capacity of the understanding.

She was born in Hanover on the 16th March 1750, the youngest but one of six children. Her exceptionally long life of nearly ninety-eight years closed in January 1848. Her memory, therefore, included the earthquake of Lisbon, the whole French Revolution, the meteor-like rise and fall of Napoleon, and all the history of modern Europe to the eve of the socialistic outbreak of 1848. Her family life, before she left Germany, was of the narrowest possible kind. She had only one sister, seventeen years older than herself; and as Sophia Herschel married early, Caroline became the only girl in her family circle, and to the full was she kept to those exclusively feminine pursuits and occupations which the proprieties of Germany at that time enforced. Her mother appears to have been enthusiastically opposed to the education of girls. Her father wished to give her a good education, but the mother insisted that nothing of the kind should be attempted. How she learned to read and write we are not told in the biography written by her grand-niece, Mrs. J. Herschel. These accomplishments were by no means common among German women of the humbler middle class a hundred years ago. She did, however, acquire them, in spite of her mother's decree that two or three months' training in the art of making household linen was all the education that Caroline required. Her father, who was a professional musician himself, wished to teach her music, but could only do so by stealth, or by taking advantage of half an hour now and then, when his wife was in an exceptionally good temper. In a letter, written when she was eighty-eight years old, Caroline recalls these furtive hours stolen from the serious occupations of her life, which then consisted in sewing, "ornamental needlework, knitting, plaiting hair, and stringing beads and bugles." "It was my lot," she writes, "tobe the Cinderella of the family.... I could never find time for improving myself in many things I knew, and which. after all, proved of no use to me afterwards, except what little I knew of music... which my father took a pleasure in teaching me—*N.B., when*

my mother was not at home. Amen."

Very early in her life her brother "William became Caroline's idol and hero. He was twelve years older than herself, and distinguished himself among the group of brothers for tenderness and kindness to the little maiden. Her eldest brother, Jacob, was a fastidious gentleman, and Caroline's inability to satisfy his requirements for nicety at table and as a waitress, often earned her a whipping. But her brother William's gentility was of a different order. She narrates one instance, which doubtless was a specimen of others, when "My dear brother William threw down his knife and fork and ran to welcome and crouched down to me, which made me forget all my grievances." Little did William or Caroline guess that in the kind brother soothing the little sister's trouble, the future astronomer was "sharpening the tool" that was hereafter to be of such inestimable service to him.

The connection of England and Hanover under one crown caused an intimate association between the two countries. William Herschel's first visit to England was as a member of the band of the regiment of which his father was bandmaster. On this first visit to England, William expended his little savings in buying Locke's "Essay on the Human Understanding." Jacob made an equally characteristic purchase of specimens of English tailoring art. These professional journeys to England led, in the course of time, to William Herschel establishing himself as a music-master and professional musican at Bath. This, however, he very early regarded merely as a means to an end. He taught music to live, but he lived for his astronomical studies and for the inventions and improvements in telescopes which he afterwards introduced to the world. When Caroline was seventeen years old, her father died, leaving his family very ill provided for; Caroline was more closely than ever confined to the tasks of a household drudge and to endeavouring to supply homemade luxuries for Jacob. This went on for five years, the mother and sister slaving night and day in order that Jacob might cut a figure in the world not humbling to the family pride. In 1772 William Herschel unexpectedly arrived from England, and his short visit ended in his sister Caroline returning with him to Bath. She left, as she writes with some awe, even after an interval of many years, "without receiving the consent of my eldest brother to my going."

There could not possibly be a greater contrast than that between Caroline's life in Hanover and her life in England. From being a maid-of-all-work in a not very interesting family, where there was a dull monotony in her daily routine of drudgery, she found she was to become a public singer, an astronomer's apprentice, and an assistant manufacturer of scientific instruments; she was not only her brother's housekeeper, but his helper and coadjutor in every act of his life. Nothing is more remarkable than the account of the life of William and Caroline Herschel at Bath. He frequently gave from thirty-five to forty musiclessons a week; this, with his work as director of public concerts, kept the wolf from the door, and, needless to say, occupied his daylight hours with tolerable completeness. The nights were given to "minding the heavens," or to making instruments necessary for minding them much more efficiently than had hitherto been possible. Every room in the house was converted into a workshop. William Herschel literally worked on, night and day, without rest, his sister on several occasions keeping him alive by putting bits of food into his mouth while he was still working. Once when he was finishing a seven-foot mirror for his telescope, he never took his hands from it for sixteen hours. The great work of constructing the forty-foot telescope took place at Bath; and at Bath also, while still practising the profession of a music-master, Herschel discovered the Georgium Sidus, and was acknowledged as the leading authority on astronomy in England.

Up to the time of Herschel's improvements, six or eight inches used to be considered a large size for the mirror of an astronomical telescope. His first great telescope had a twelve-foot mirror. There is a most exciting account in

Mrs. Herschel's Life of Caroline Herschel, of the failure of the first casting of the mirror for the thirty-foot reflector. The molten metal leaked from the vessel containing it and fell on the stone floor, pieces of which flew about in all directions as high as the ceiling. The operators fortunately escaped without serious injury. "My poor brother fell, exhausted with heat and exertion, on a heap of brickbats." The disappointment must have been intense, but nothing ever baffled these indefatigable workers, and the second casting was a complete success.

Five years after she had joined her brother at Bath, Caroline made her first appearance as a public singer. She was very successful, and her friends anticipated that her well-cultivated and beautiful voice would become a means of providing her with an ample income. She, however, had so fully identified herself with her brother's astronomical labours, that she only regarded her musical acquirements as a means of setting him free to devote himself more completely to the real object of his life. His fame as a maker of telescopes had by this time spread all over Europe, and many scientific societies, royal persons, and other celebrities, ordered telescopes of him. On these orders he was able to realise a large profit, but Caroline always grudged the time devoted to their execution. Her aim for her brother was not that he should become rich or even well-to-do, but that he should devote himself unreservedly to advance the progress of astronomical science. She was ready to live on a crust, and to give herself up to the most pinching economies and even privations, for this end. She was the keeper of her brother's purse, and received his commands to spend therefrom anything that was necessary for herself; her thrift and self-denial may be judged from the fact that the sum thus abstracted for her own personal wants seldom amounted to more than £7 or £8 a year.

The next great change in the life of the brother and sister took place in 1782, when William Herschel left Bath and was appointed Astronomer-Koyal

by George the Third. His salary of only £200 a year involved a great loss of income, but this, in his eyes, was a small matter in comparison with the advantage of having his time entirely free to give up to his favourite studies. They bade farewell to Bath, and settled first at Datchet, shortly after, however, removing to Slough. Caroline had dismal visions of bankruptcy, but William was in the highest spirits, and declared that they would live on eggs and bacon, "which would cost nothing to speak of, now that they were really in the country."

Caroline was now installed as an assistant astronomer, and was given a telescope, which she calls a "seven-foot Newtonian Sweeper "; and she was instructed, whenever she had an evening not in attendance on her brother, to "sweep for comets "; but her principal business appears, at this time, to have been waiting on her brother, and writing down the results of his observations; they worked quite as hard as they had done at Bath. They laboured at the manufacture of instruments all day, and at the observation of the heavens all night. No severity of weather, if the sky was clear, ever kept them from their posts. The ink often froze with which Caroline was writing down the results of her brother's observations. It has been well said that if it had not been for occasional cloudy nights, they must have died of overwork. The apparatus for erecting the great forty-foot telescope, and the iron and woodwork for its various motions, were all designed by William Herschel, and fixed under his immediate direction. His sister, in her *Eecollections,* wrote: "I have seen him stretched many an hour in the burning sun across the top beam, whilst the iron-work for the various motions was being fixed." The penurious salary granted to William Herschel was supplemented by special grants for the removal and the erection of all this machinery; and in 1787 Caroline's services to her brother were publicly recognised by her receiving the appointment of assistant to her brother at a salary of £50 a year. She was at all times grateful to members of the royal family for acts of kindness shown by them to her brother and herself; but it is evident that she felt that, so far as money was concerned, she had not much cause for gratitude to the royal bounty. She points out that at the time when Parliament was granting George III. the sum of £80,000 a year for encouraging science, £200 was considered a sufficient salary for the first astronomer of the day; and yet money could flow liberally enough in some directions, for £30,000 was at that time being spent on the altar-piece of St. George's Chapel, Windsor. Even Caroline's little salary of £50 a year was not regularly paid. It was a trial to her again to become a pensioner on her brother's purse, and it was not till nine quarters of her official salary remained unpaid, that she reluctantly applied to him for help. No wonder that in reading, after her brother's death, an account of his life and its achievements, she remarks, "The favours of monarchs ought to have been mentioned, *but once would have been enough.*"

It was after her brother's marriage, in 1788, that the majority of Caroline's astronomical discoveries were made. She discovered her first comet in 1786, her eighth and last in 1797. She was recognised as a comrade by all the leading astronomers of Europe, and received many letters complimenting her on her discoveries. One from De la Lande addressed her as "Savante Miss," while another from the Rev. Dr. Maskelyne saluted her as "My worthy sister in astronomy." Royal and other distinguished visitors constantly visited the wonderful forty-foot telescope at Slough, and either William Herschel or his sister were required to be in attendance to explain its marvels. The Prince of Orange, on one occasion, called, and left an extraordinary message "to ask Mr. Herschel, or if he was not at home, Miss Herschel, if it was true that Mr. Herschel had discovered a new star, whose light was not as that of the common stars, but with swallow-tails, as stars in embroidery." The only glimpse we get, through the peaceful labours of Caroline's long life, of the strife and

turmoil of the French Revolution, is the note she makes of the visit, to her brother's observatory, of the Princesse de Lamballe. "About a fortnight after this," the diarist observes, "her head was off. " The absence of all comment upon the wonderful political events of the time is noticeable, and so also is Caroline's thinly-veiled contempt for any science less sublime than that to which she and her brother were devoted. Her youngest brother, Dietrich, was a student of the insect world. "He amuses himself with insects," she wrote to her nephew; "it is well he does not see the word *amuses,* for whenever he catches a fly with a leg more than usual, he says it is as good as catching a comet." Her brother's marriage, though far from welcome at the time it took place, was a great blessing to her; for it gave her a most tender and affectionate sister, and ultimately a nephew, the inheritor of his father's great gifts, and the being to whom, after William Herschel's death in 1822, Caroline transferred all the devoted and passionate attachment of which her nature was capable.

The great mistake of her life was going back to Germany after Sir W. Herschel's death in 1822. She was then seventy-two years of age, and the previous fifty years of her life, containing all her most precious memories and associations, had been spent in England. In this country, also, were all those who were dearest to her. Yet, no sooner was her brother dead, than she felt life in England to be an impossibility. She little thought that she had still twenty-six years to live; indeed she had long been under the impression that her end was near, but while her brother lived she kept this to herself, because she wished to be useful to him as long as she possibly could. She never really re-acclimatised herself to Germany. "Why did I leave happy England?" she often said. The one German institution she thoroughly enjoyed was the winter series of concerts and operas, which she constantly attended, and she mentions with pleasure, in her letters, that she was "always sure to be noticed by the Duke of Cambridge as his countrywoman, and

that is what I want; I will be no Hanoverian." She laments the death of William IV., chiefly because, by causing a separation of the crowns of England and Hanover, it seemed to break a link between herself and the country of her adoption.

She never revisited England, but she kept up a constant communication with it by letters to her sister-in-law, her nephew, and later to her niece, Sir John Herschel's wife. At that time the post between London and Hanover was an affair of fifteen days, and letters were carried by a monthly messenger, of whose services she seldom failed to avail herself. She took the keenest interest in her nephew's distinguished career. His letters to her are full of astronomy. In 1832 he made a voyage to the Cape to observe the stars in the Southern Hemisphere. When Miss Herschel first heard of the intended voyage she refused to believe it. But when she was really convinced of it, the old impulse was as strong upon her as upon a warhorse who hears the trumpet. "Ja! if I was thirty or forty years younger and could go too!" she exclaimed.

On 1st January 1840 the tube of the celebrated fortyfoot telescope was closed with a sort of family celebration. A requiem, composed by Sir John Herschel for the occasion, was chanted, and he and Lady Herschel, with their seven children and some old servants, walked in procession round it, singing as they went. On hearing of this from Slough, Miss Herschel recalls that the famous telescope had also been inaugurated with music. "God save the King" had then been sung in it, the whole company from the dinnertable mounting into the tube, and taking any musical instruments they could get hold of, to form a band and orchestra.

The most laborious of all her undertakings she accomplished after her brother's death. It was "The Reduction and Arrangement in the form of a catalogue, in Zones, of all the Star Clusters and Nebulae, observed by Sir W. Herschel in hi3 Sweeps." It was for this that the gold medal of the Royal Astronomical Society was voted to her in 1828.

All through her life in Hanover she lived with the most careful economy, seldom or never consenting to draw upon Sir John Herschel for the annuity of £100 that had been left her by her brother. She said it was impossible for her to spend more than £50 a year without making herself ridiculous. The only luxuries she granted herself were her concert and opera tickets, and her English bed, which all sufferers from the inhuman German bedding must be thankful to hear she possessed. The self-forgetfulness and devotion to others which had characterised her in youth accompanied her to her grave. Every detail with regard to the disposition of her property and the arrangements for her funeral had been made by herself, with the view of giving as little trouble as possible to her nephew, and making the smallest encroachment upon his time. In her latest moments her only thought for herself was embodied in a request that a lock of her beloved brother's hair might be laid with her in her coffin.

SARAH MARTIN THE DRESSMAKER AND PRISON VISITOR OF YARMOUTH

"Two men I honour and no third. First the toilwom craftsman that with earthmade Implement laboriously conquers the earth and makes her man's.... A second man I honour, and still more highly: Him who is seen toiling for the spiritually indispensable; not daily bread, but the bread of Life.... Unspeakably touching is it however when I find both dignities united; and he that must toil outwardly for the lowest of man's wants, is also toiling inwardly for the highest. Sublimer in this world know I nothing than the Peasant Saint, could such now anywhere be met with. Such a one will take thee back to Nazareth itself; thou wilt see the splendour of Heaven spring forth from the humblest depths of Earth, like a light shining in great darkness."— *Sartor Eesartus,* pp. 157, 158.

Every one of us has probably been tempted at one time or another to say or think when asked to join in some good work, "If only I had more time or more money, I would take it up." It is good for us, therefore, to be reminded that neither leisure nor wealth are necessary to those whose hearts are fixed upon the earnest desire to leave this world a little better and a little happier than they found it.

This lesson was wonderfully taught by Sarah Martin, a poor dressmaker, who was born at Caister, near Great Yarmouth, in 1791. In her own locality she did as great a work in solving the problems of prison discipline, and how to improve the moral condition of prisoners, as Mrs. Fry was doing about the same time upon a larger scale in London. It is very extraordinary that this poor woman, who was almost entirely self-educated, and who was dependent on daily toil for daily bread, should have been able, through her own mother-wit and native goodness of heart, to see the evil and provide the same remedies for it as were in course of time provided throughout the land, as the result of study given to the subject, by statesmen, philosophers, and philanthropists.

When Sarah Martin first began to visit the prison at Great Yarmouth, there was no sort of provision for the moral or educational improvement of the prisoners. There was no chaplain, there were no religious services, there was no school, and there was no employment of any kind, except what Satan finds for idle hands to do. The quiet, little, gentle-voiced dressmaker changed all this.

She was first led to visit the prison in 1819, through the compassionate horror which filled her when she heard of the committal to prison of a woman for brutally illtreating her child. Without any introduction or recommendation from influential persons, she knocked timidly at the gate of the prison, and asked leave to see this woman. She had not told a single human creature of her intention, not even her grandmother, with whom she lived. She was fearful lest she should be overcome by the counsels of worldly wisdom that she had better mind her own business, that the woman's wickedness was no concern of hers, and so forth. Her first application at the gaol was unsuccessful; but she tried again, and the second time she was admitted without any question whatever. Once in the presence of the prisoner, the first inquiry by which she was met was a somewhat rough one as to the object of her visit. When the poor creature heard and felt all the deep compassion which had moved Sarah Martin to her side, she burst into tears, and with many expressions of contrition and gratitude besought her visitor to help her to be a better woman.

From the date of this visit, the best energies of Sarah Martin's life were devoted to improving the lot of the prisoners in Great Yarmouth Gaol. She did not—indeed, she could not—give up her dressmaking. She worked out at her customers' houses, earning about Is. 3d. a day. Her first resolve was to give up always one day a week to her prison work, and as many other days as she could spare. She began teaching the prisoners to read and write; she also read to them, and told them stories. A deeply religious woman herself, it pained her that there were no services of any kind in the prison, and she prevailed upon the prisoners to gather together on Sunday mornings and read to one another. To encourage them in this she attended herself, not at first as the conductor of the service, but as a fellow-worshipper. This was very typical of her method and character. She was among them as one who served, not as one seeking power and authority. Another illustration of this sweet humility in her character may be given. She wished those of her pupils who could read to learn each day a few Bible texts; and she always learned some herself, and said them with the prisoners. Sometimes an objection was made. In her own words, "Many said at first, 'It would be of no use,' and my reply was, 'It is of use to me, and why should it not be so to you? You have not tried it, but I have.'" There was a simplicity in this, a complete absence of the "Depart from me, for I am holier than thou," which was irresistible, and always silenced excuse.

Soon after the commencement of the Sunday services in the prison, it was found necessary, through the difficulty of finding a reader, that Sarah Martin herself should conduct the service. At first she used to read a sermon from a book, but later she wrote her own sermons, and later still she was able to preach without writing beforehand. According to the testimony of Captain Williams, the Inspector of Prisons for the district, the whole service was in a high degree reverent and impressive. The prisoners listened with deep attention to the clear, melodious voice of their self-appointed pastor.

At no time did she seek to obtain from the governor of the prison any authority over the prisoners; that is, she never sought to control them against their will; authority over them she had, but it was the authority which proceeded from her own personal influence. The prisoners did what she wished, because they knew her devotion to them. Her hold over them is best proved by the fact that never but once did she meet from them with anything that could be called rudeness or insult.

Next to her care for godliness and education, her chief thoughts were given to provide employment for the prisoners, first for the women, and then for the men. A gentleman gave her 10s., and in the same week another gave her £1. Her gratitude for the possession of this small capital is touching to read of. She expended it in the purchase of materials for baby-clothes, and borrowing patterns, she set the women to work upon making little shifts and wrappers. The garments, when completed, were sold for the benefit of the women who had made them.

Her capital grew from thirty shillings to seven guineas, and in all more than £400 worth of clothing, made in this way, was sold. The advantages were twofold. First, the women were employed and taught to sew, and secondly, each woman was enabled to earn a small sum, which was saved for her till the time of her release from prison. This money was frequently the means of giving the discharged prisoner a chance of starting a new life and gaining an honest livelihood.

Sarah Martin gave particular attention to this very important branch of her work. A man or a woman just out of prison, branded with all the stigma and disgrace of the gaol, is too often almost forced back into crime as the only means of livelihood. Endless were the devices and schemes which Sarah Martin employed to prevent this. She would seek out respectable lodgings for the prisoners on their discharge; she would see their former employers and entreat that another chance might be given; her notebooks and diaries are filled with items of her own personal expenditure in setting up her poor clients with the small stock-in-trade or the tools necessary to start some simple business on their own account.

After many years of patient and devoted work she was well known throughout the whole town and neighbourhood, and was no longer entirely dependent on her own slender earnings. Her grandmother died in 1826, and she then inherited a small income of about £12 a year. She removed into Yarmouth, and hired two rooms in a poor part of the town. Shortly after this she entirely gave up working as a dressmaker. She could not, of course, live on the little annuity she inherited from her grandmother; this was not much more than enough to pay for her rooms. But she did not fear for herself. Her personal wants were of the simplest description, and she said herself that she had no care: "God, who had called me into the vineyard, had said, 'Whatsoever is right, I will give you.'" It would, indeed, have been to the discredit of Yarmouth if such a woman had been suffered to be in want. Many gifts were sent to her, but she scrupulously devoted everything that reached her to the prisoners, unless the donor expressly stated that it was not for her charities but for herself. About 1840, after twenty-one years' work in the prison and workhouse of the town, the Corporation of Yarmouth urged her to accept a small salary from the borough funds. She at first refused, because it was painful to her that the prisoners should ever regard her in any other light than as their disinterested friend; she feared that if she accepted the money of the Corporation she would be looked upon as merely one of the gaol functionaries, and that they would "rank her with the turnkeys and others who got their living by the duties which they discharged." It was urged upon her that this view was a mistaken one, and she was advised at least to accept a small salary as an experiment. She replied, "To try the experiment, which might injure the thing I live and breathe for, seems like

D applying a knife to your child's throat to know if it will cut. As for my circumstances, I have not a wish ungratified, and am more than content." The following year, however, it was evident that her health was giving way, and another attempt was made, which ended in the Corporation voting her the small sum of £12 a year, not as a salary, but as a voluntary gift to one who had been of such inestimable service to the town. She did not live long after this. Her health gradually became feebler, but she continued her daily work at the gaol till 17th April 1843. After that date she never again left her rooms, and after a few months of intense suffering, she died on the 15th October. When the nurse who was with her told her the end was near, she clasped her hands together and exclaimed, "Thank God, thank God." They were her last words. She was buried at Caister; the tombstone which marks her grave bears an inscription dictated by herself, giving simply her name and the dates of her birth and death, with a reference to the chapter of Corinthians which forms part of the Church of England Service for the Burial of the Dead. Well, indeed, is it near that grave, and full of the thoughts inspired by that life, for us to feel that "Death is swallowed up in victory."

The citizens of Yarmouth marked their gratitude and veneration for her by putting a stained-glass window to her memory in St. Nicholas's Church. Her name is reverently cherished in her native town. Dr. Stanley, who was Bishop of Norwich at the time of her death, gave expression to the general feeling when he said, "I would canonise Sarah Martin if I could !" MARY SOMERVILLE

Mary Somerville, the most remarkable scientific woman our country has produced, was born at Jedburgh in 1780. Her father was a naval officer, and in December 1780 had just parted from his wife to go on foreign service for some years. She had accompanied her husband to London, and on returning home to Scotland was obliged to stay at the Manse of Jedburgh, the home of her brother-in-law and sister, Dr. and Mrs. Somerville. Here little Mary was born, in the house of her uncle and aunt, who afterwards became her father and mother-in-law, for her second husband was their son. In the interesting reminiscences she has left of her life, she records the curious fact that she was born in the home of her future husband, and was nursed by his mother.

Mary was of good birth on both sides. Her father was Admiral Sir William Fairfax, of the well-known Yorkshire family of that name, which had furnished a General to the Parliamentary army in the civil wars of the reign of Charles I. This family was connected with that of the famous American patriot, George Washington. During the American War of Independence, Mary Somerville's father, then Lieutenant Fairfax, was on board his ship on an American station, when he received a letter from General Washington, claiming cousinship with him, and inviting the young man to pay him a visit. The invitation was not accepted, but Lieutenant Fairfax's daughter lived to regret that the letter which conveyed it had not been preserved. Admiral Fairfax was concerned with Admiral Duncan in the famous victory of Camperdown, and gave many proofs that he was in every way a gallant sailor and a brave man. Mary Somerville's mother was of an ancient Scottish family named Charters. The pride of descent was very strongly marked among her Scotch relatives. Lady Fairfax does not seem much to have sympathised with her remarkable child. Mary, however, inherited some excellent qualities from both parents. Lady Fairfax was, in some ways, as courageous as her husband; notwithstanding a full allowance of Scotch superstitions and a special terror of storms and darkness, she had what her daughter

called "presence of mind and the courage of necessity." On one occasion the house she was living in was in the greatest danger of being burned down. The flames of a neighbouring fire had spread till they reached the next house but one to that which she occupied. Casks of turpentine and oil in a neighbouring carriage manufactory were exploding with the heat. Lady Fairfax made all the needful preparations for saving her furniture, and had her family plate and papers securely packed. She assembled in the house a sufficient number of men to move the furniture out, if needs were. Then she quietly remarked, "Now let us breakfast; it is time enough for us to move our things when the next house takes fire." The next house, after all, did not take fire, and, while her neighbours lost half their property by throwing it recklessly into the street, before the actual necessity for doing so had arisen, Lady Fairfax suffered no loss at all. The same kind of cool courage was often exhibited by Mary Somerville in later life. On one occasion she stayed with her family at Florence during a severe outbreak of cholera there, when almost every one who could do so had fled panic-stricken from the city.

During the long absences of Sir William Fairfax on foreign service, Lady Fairfax and her children led a very quiet life at the little seaside village of Burntisland, just opp6site to Edinburgh, on the Firth of Forth. As a young child, Mary led a wild, outdoor life, with hardly any education, in the ordinary sense of the word, though there is no doubt that in collecting shells, fossils, and seaweeds, in watching and studying the habits and appearance of wild birds, and in gazing at the stars through her little bedroom window, the whole life of this wonderful child was really an education of the great powers of her mind. However, when her father returned from sea about 1789 he was shocked to find Mary "such a little savage"; and it was resolved that she must be sent to a boarding school. She remained there a year and learned nothing at all. Her lithesome, active, well-formed body

was enclosed in stiff stays, with a steel busk in front; a metal rod, with a semicircle which went under the chin, was clasped to this busk, and in this instrument of torture she was set to learn columns of Johnson's dictionary by heart. This was the process which at that time went by the name of education in girls' schools. Fortunately she was not kept long at school. Mary had learned nothing, and her mother was angry that she had spent so much money in vain. She would have been content, she said, if Mary had only learnt to write well and keep accounts, which was all that a woman was expected to know. After this Mary soon commenced the process of self-education which only ended with her long life of ninety-two years. She not only learnt all she could about birds, beasts, fishes, plants, eggs and seaweeds, but she also found a Shakespeare which she read at every moment when she could do so undisturbed. A little later her mother moved into Edinburgh for the winter, and Mary had music lessons, and by degrees taught herself Latin. The studious bent of her mind had now thoroughly declared itself; but till she was about fourteen she had never received a word of encouragement about her studies. At that age she had the good fortune to pay a visit to her uncle and aunt at Jedburgh, in whose house she had been born. Her uncle, Dr. Somerville, was the first person who ever encouraged and helped her in her studies. She ventured to confide in him that she had been trying to learn Latin by herself, but feared it was no use. lie reassured her by telling her of the women in ancient times who had been classical scholars. He moreover read Virgil with her for two hours every morning in his study. A few years later than this she taught herself Greek enough to read Xenophon and Herodotus, and in time she became sufficiently proficient in the language to thoroughly appreciate its greatest literature.

One of the most striking things about her was the manysided character of her mind. Some people—men as well as women—who. are scientific or mathematical seem to care for nothing but science or mathematics; but it may be truly said of her that "Everything was grist that came to her mill." There was hardly any branch of art or knowledge which she did not delight in. She studied painting under Mr. Nasmyth in Edinburgh, and he declared her to be the best pupil he had ever had. Almost to the day of her death she delighted in painting and drawing. She was also an excellent musician and botanist. The special study with which her name will always be associated was mathematics as applied to the study of the heavens, but she also wrote on physical geography and on microscopic science. It is sometimes thought that if women are learned they are nearly sure to neglect their domestic duties, or that, in the witty words of Sydney Smith, "if women are permitted to eat of the tree of knowledge, the rest of the family will soon be reduced to the same aerial and unsatisfactory diet. " Mrs. Somerville was a living proof of the folly of this opinion. She was an excellent housewife and a particularly skilful needlewoman. She astonished those who thought a scientific woman could not understand anything of cookery, by her notable preparation of black currant jelly for her husband's throat on their wedding journey. On one occasion she supplied with marmalade, made by her own hands, one of the ships that were being fitted out for a Polar expedition. She was a most loving wife and tender mother as well as a devoted and faithful friend. She gave up far more time than most mothers do to the education of her children. Her love of animals, especially of birds, was very strongly developed. With all her devotion to science she was horrified at the barbarities of vivisection, and cordially supported those who have successfully exerted themselves to prevent it from spreading in England to the same hideous proportions which it has reached on the continent of Europe. Many pages of one of her learned works were written with a little tame mountain sparrow sitting on her shoulder. On one occasion, having been introduced to the Hon. Mountstuart Elphinstone, she says

he quite won her heart by exclaiming, in reference to the number of little birds that were eaten in Italy, "What! robins! Eat a robin! I would as soon eat a child. "

Her first husband, Mr. Samuel Greig, only lived three years after their marriage in 1804. He appears to have been one of those men of inferior capacity, who dislike and dread intellectual power in women. He had a very low opinion of the intelligence of women, and had himself no interest in, nor knowledge of, any kind of science. When his wife was left a widow with two sons at the early age of twenty-seven, she returned to her father's house in Scotland, and worked steadily at mathematics. She profited by the instructions of Professor Wallace, of the University of Edinburgh, and gained a silver medal from one of the mathematical societies of that day. Nearly all the members of her family were still loud in their condemnation of what they chose to regard as her eccentric and foolish behaviour in devoting herself to science instead of society. There were, however, exceptions. Her Uncle and Aunt Somerville and their son William did not join in the chorus of disapprobation which her studies provoked. With them she found a real home of loving sympathy and encouragement. In 1812 she and her cousin William were married. His delight and pride in her during their long married life of nearly fifty years were unbounded. For the first time in her life she now had the daily companionship of a thoroughly sympathetic spirit Much of what the world owes to her it owes indirectly to him, because he stimulated her powers, and delighted in anything that brought them out. He was in the medical department of the army, and scientific pursuits were thoroughly congenial to him. He had a fine and well cultivated mind which he delighted in using to further his wife's pursuits. He searched libraries for the books she required, "copying and recopying her manuscripts to save her time." In the words of one of their daughters, "No trouble seemed too great which he bestowed upon her; it was a labour of love.

" When Mrs. Somerville became famous through her scientific writings, the other members of her family, who had formerly ridiculed and blamed her, became loud in her praise. She knew how to value such commendation in comparison with that which she had constantly received from her husband. She wrote about this, "The warmth with which my husband entered into my success deeply affected me; for not one in ten thousand would have rejoiced at it as he did; but he was of a generous nature, far above jealousy, and he continued through life to take the kindest interest in all I did." Mrs. Somerville's first work, *The Mechanism of the Heavens,* would probably never have been written but at the instance of Lord Brougham, whose efforts were warmly supported by those of Mr. Somerville. In March 1827 Lord Brougham, on behalf of the Society for the Diffusion of Useful Knowledge, wrote a letter begging Mrs. Somerville to write an account of Newton's *Principia* and of La Place's *Mdcanique CMeste.* In reference to the latter book he wrote, "In England there are now not twenty people who know this great work, except by name, and not a hundred who know it even by name. My firm belief is that Mrs. Somerville could add two cyphers to each of these figures." Mrs. Somerville was overwhelmed with astonishment at this request. She was most modest and diffident of her own powers, and honestly believed that her self-acquired knowledge was so greatly inferior to that of the men who had been educated at the universities, that it would be the height of presumption for her to attempt to write on the subject. The persuasions of Lord Brougham and of her husband at last prevailed so far that she promised to make the attempt; on the express condition, however, that her manuscript should be put into the fire unless it fulfilled the expectations of those who urged its production. "Thus suddenly," she writes, "the whole character and course of my future life was changed." One is tempted to believe that this first plunge into authorship was, to some extent, stimulated by a loss of nearly all their fortune which had a short time before befallen Mr. and Mrs. Somerville. Before authorship has become a habit, the whip of poverty is often needed to rouse a student to the exertion and labour it requires. The impediments to authorship in Mrs. Somerville's case were more than usually formidable. In the memoirs she has left of this part of her life, she speaks of the difficulty which she experienced as the mother of a family and the head of a household in keeping any time free for her work. It was only after she had attended to social and family duties that she had time for writing, and even then she was subjected to many interruptions. The Somervilles were then living at Chelsea, and she felt at that distance from town, it would be ungracious to decline to receive those who had come out to call upon her. But she groans at the remembrance of the annoyance she sometimes felt when she was engaged in solving a difficult problem, by the entry of a well-meaning friend, who would calmly announce, "I have come to spend an hour or two with you." Her work, to which she gave the name of *The Mechanism of the Heavens,* progressed, however, in spite of interruptions, to such good purpose that in less than a year it was complete, and it immediately placed its author in the first rank among the scientific thinkers and writers of the day. She was elected an honorary member of the Astronomical Society, at the same time with Caroline Herschel, and honours and rewards of all kinds flowed in upon her. Her bust, by Chan trey, was placed in the great hall of the Royal Society, and she was elected an honorary member of the Royal Academy of Dublin, and of many other scientific societies. It was a little later than this, in 1835, that Sir Robert Peel, on behalf of the Government, conferred a civil list pension of £200 a year upon Mrs. Somerville; the announcement of this came almost simultaneously with the news of the loss of the remainder of her own and her husband's private fortune, through the treachery of those who had been entrusted with it. The public recognition of her services to science

came therefore at a very appropriate time; the pension was a few years later increased to '£300 a year by Lord John Russell.

Throughout her life Mrs. Somerville was a staunch advocate of all that tended to raise up and improve the lot of women. When quite a young girl she was stimulated to work hard by the feeling that it was in her power thus to serve the cause of her fellow-women. Writing of the period when she was only sixteen years old, she says: "I must say the idea of making money had never entered my head in any of my pursuits, but I was intensely ambitious to excel in something, for I felt in my own breast that women were capable of taking a higher place in creation than that assigned to them in my early days, which was very low." It is interesting to observe that her enthusiasm for what are sometimes called "women's rights" was as warm at the end of her life as it had been at its dawn. When she was eighty-nine, she was as keen as she had been at sixteen for all that lifts up the lot of women. She was a firm supporter of Mr. John Stuart Mill in the effort he made to extend to women the benefit and protection of Parliamentary representation. She recognised that many of the English laws are unjust to women, and clearly saw that there can be no security for their being made just and equal until the law-makers are chosen partly by women and partly by men. The first name to the petition in favour of women's suffrage which was presented to Parliament by Mr. J. S. Mill in 1868 was that of Mary Somerville. She also joined in the first petition to the Senate of the London University, praying that degrees might be granted to women. At the time this petition was unsuccessful, but its prayer was granted within a very few years. One cannot but regret that Mrs. Somerville did not live to see this fulfilment of her wishes. She showed her sympathy with the movement for the higher education of women, by bequeathing her mathematical and scientific library to Girton College. It is one of the possessions of which the College is most justly proud. The books are en-

closed in a very beautifully designed case, which also forms a sort of framework for a cast of Chantrey's bust of Mrs. Somerville. The fine and delicate lines of her beautiful face offer to the students of the College a worthy ideal of completely developed womanhood, in which intellect and emotion balance one another and make a perfect whole.

Mrs. Somerville's other works, written after *The Mechanism of the Heavens,* were *The Connection of the Physical Sciences, Physical Geography,* and *Molecular and Microscopic Science.* The last book was commenced after she had completed her eightieth year. Her mental powers remained unimpaired to a remarkably late period, and she also had extraordinary physical vigour to the end of her life. She affords a striking instance of the fallacy of supposing that intellectual labour undermines the physical strength of women. Her last occupations, continued till the actual day of her death, were the revision and completion of a treatise on *The Theory of Differences,* and the study of a book on *Quaternions.* Her only physical infirmity in extreme old age was deafness. She was able to go out and enjoy life up to the time of her death, which took place in 1872, at the great age of ninety-two years.

She was a woman of deep and strong religious feeling. Her beautiful character shines through every word and action of her life. Her deep humility was very striking, as was also her tenderness for, and her sympathy with, the sufferings of all who were wretched and oppressed. One of the last entries in her journal refers again to her love of animals, and she says, "Among the numerous plans for the education of the young, let us hope that mercy may be taught as a part of religion." The reflections in these last pages of her diary give such a lovely picture of serene, noble, and dignified old age that they may well be quoted here. They show the warm heart of the generous woman, as well as the trained intellect of a reverent student of the laws of nature. "Though far advanced in years, I take as lively an interest as ever in passing events. I regret that I shall not live to know the result of the expedition to determine the currents of the ocean, the distance of the earth from the sun determined by the transits of Venus, and the source of the most renowned of rivers, the discovery of which will immortalise the name of Dr. Livingstone. But I regret most of all that I shall not see the suppression of the most atrocious system of slavery that ever disgraced humanity—that made known to the world by Dr. Livingstone and by Mr. Stanley, and which Sir Bartle Frere has gone to suppress, by order of the British Government." A later entry still, and the last, gives another view of her happy, faithful spirit. The Admiral's daughter speaks in it: "The Blue Peter has been long flying at my foremast, and now that I am in my ninety-second year I must soon expect the signal for sailing. It is a solemn voyage, but it does not disturb my tranquility. Deeply sensible of my utter unworthiness, and profoundly grateful for the innumerable blessings I have received, I trust in the infinite mercy of my Almighty Creator." She then expresses her gratitude for the loving care of her daughters, and her journal concludes with the words, "I am perfectly happy." She died and was buried at Naples. Her death took place in her sleep, on 29th November 1872. Her daughter writes, "Her pure spirit passed away so gently that those around her scarcely perceived when she left them. It was the beautiful and painless close of a noble and happy life." Wordsworth's words about old age were fully realised in her case—

Thy thoughts and feelings shall not die,
Nor leave thee when gray hairs are nigh,
A melancholy slave;
But an old age, serene and bright,
And lovely as a Lapland night,
  Shall lead thee to thy grave.

VI QUEEN VICTORIA

A Jubilee, or a fiftieth anniversary of the reign of a king or queen, is a very rare event in our history. Rather more than a thousand years have rolled away since the time when Egbert was the first king of all England. And in all these thousand years there have only been

three jubilees before that now celebrated, and these three have each been clouded by some national or personal misfortune casting a gloom over the rejoicings which would naturally have taken place on such an occasion. It is rather curious that each of the three kings of England who has reached a fiftieth year of sovereignty has been the third of his name to occupy the throne. Henry III., Edward III., and George III. are the only English sovereigns, before Victoria, who have reigned for as long as fifty years. In the case of Henry the Third, the fifty years of his reign are a record of bad government, rebellion, and civil war. Edward the Third's reign, which began so triumphantly, ended in disaster; the king had fallen into a kind of dotage; Edward the Black Prince had died before his father, and the kingdom was ruled by the incompetent and unscrupulous John of Gaunt; the last years of this reign were characterised by military disasters, by harsh and unjust methods of taxation, and by subservience to the Written for the Jubilee, June 1887. papacy. Those who thus sowed the wind were not long in reaping the whirlwind; for these misfortunes were followed by the one hundred years' war with France, by the peasants' war under Wat Tyler, and by the persecution of heretics in England, when for the first time in our history a statute was passed forfeiting the lives of men and women for their religious opinions. Passing on to the reign of George III., the jubilee of 1810 must have been a sad one, for the poor king had twice had attacks of madness, and one of exceptional severity began in the very year of the jubilee. Happily, on the present occasion the spell is broken. The Queen is not the third, but the first of her name, and although there are no doubt many causes for anxiety as regards the outlook in our political and social history, yet there are still greater causes for hopefulness and for confidence that the marvellous improvement in the social, moral, and material condition of the people which has marked the reign in the past will be continued in the future.

It is not very easy at this distance of

time to picture to one's self the passion of loyalty and devotion inspired by the young girl who became Queen of England in 1837. To realise what was felt for her, one must look at the character of the monarchs who had immediately preceded her. The immorality and faithlessness of George IV. are too well known to need emphasis. He was probably one of the most contemptible human beings who ever occupied a throne; he was eaten up by vanity, self-indulgence, and grossness. With no pretence to conjugal fidelity himself, he attempted to visit with the severest punishment the supposed infidelity of the unhappy woman who had been condemned to be his wife. Recklessly extravagant where his own glorification or pleasure was concerned, he could be penurious enough to a former boon companion who had fallen into want. There is hardly a feature in his character, either as a man or a sovereign, that could win genuine esteem or love. Mrs. Somerville was present at the gorgeous scene of his coronation, when something more than a quarter of a million of money was spent in decorations and ceremonial. She describes the tremendous effect produced upon every one by the knocking at the door which announced that Queen Caroline was claiming admittance. She says every heart stood still; it was like the handwriting on the wall at Belshazzar's feast. Only by contrast with such a man as George IV. could William IV. be regarded with favour. Several prominent offices about the Court were occupied by the Fitz Clarences, his illegitimate children. His manners were described as "bluff" by those who wished to make the best of them; "brutal" would have been a more accurate word. On one occasion a guest at one of his dinner parties asked for water, and the king, with an oath, exclaimed that no water should be drunk at his table. On another occasion, on his birthday, he took the opportunity, in the presence of the young Princess Victoria and her mother, the Duchess of Kent, to make the most unmanly and ungenerous attack upon the latter, who was sitting by his side. Greville speaks of this outburst as an extraordinary and outrageous speech. The Princess burst into tears, and her mother rose and ordered her carriage for her immediate departure.

It is no wonder that the Duchess of Kent was anxious, as far as possible, to keep her daughter from the influence of such a Court as this. Much of the Queen's conscientiousness and punctual discharge of the political duties of her station may be attributed to her careful education by her mother and her uncle Leopold, the widower of Princess Charlotte, and afterwards King of the Belgians. It is not possible to tell from the published memorials what clouds overshadowed the Princess Victoria's childhood. She seems to have had a most loving mother, excellent health and abilities, and a judicious training in every way; yet she says herself, in reference to the choice of the name of Leopold for her youngest son, "It is a name which is the dearest to me after Albert, one which recalls the almost only happy days of my sad childhood."

It is evident, therefore, that her young life was not so happy and tranquil as it appeared to be to outsiders. Perhaps her extreme and almost abnormal sense of responsibility was hardly compatible with the joyousness of childhood. There is a story that it was not till the Princess was eleven years old that her future destiny was revealed to her. Her governess then purposely put a genealogical table of the royal family into her history book. The child gazed earnestly at it, and by degrees she comprehended what it meant, namely, that she herself was next in succession to the ancient crown of England; she put her hand into her governess's and said, "I will be good. I understand now why you wanted me to learn so much, even Latin.... I understand all better now." And she repeated more than once, "I will be good." The anecdote shows an unusually keen sense of duty and of conscientiousness in so young a child, and there are other anecdotes which show the same characteristic. Who, therefore, can wonder at the unbounded joy which filled all hearts in England when this young girl,

pure, sweet, innocent, conscientious, and unselfish, ascended the throne of George IV. and William IV. / Her manners were frank, natural, simple, and dignified. The bright young presence of the girl Queen filled every one, high and low, throughout the nation with enthusiasm.

The American author, Mr. N. P. Willis, republican as he was, spoke of her in one of his letters as "quite unnecessarily pretty and interesting for the heir of such a crown as that of England." Daniel O'Connell, then the leader of the movement for the repeal of the union between England and Ireland, was as great an enthusiast for her as any one in the three kingdoms. His stentorian voice led the cheering of the crowd outside of St. James's Palace who welcomed her at the ceremony of proclamation. He said, when some of the gossips of the day chattered of a scheme to depose "the all but infant Queen" in favour of the hated Duke of Cumberland, "If necessary I can get 500,000 brave Irishmen to defend the life, the honour, and the person of the beloved young lady by whom England's throne is now filled."

E

The picture of the Queen's first council by Wilkie was shown in 1887 in the winter exhibition at the Royal Academy. It helps one very much to understand the sort of enthusiasm which she created. The sweet, girlish dignity and quiet simplicity with which she performed all the duties of her station filled every one with admiration. Surrounded by aged politicians, statesmen, and soldiers, she presides over them all with the grace and dignity associated with a complete absence of affectation and self-consciousness. Greville, the Clerk of the Council then, and for many years before and after, writes of this occasion: "Never was anything like the impression she produced, or the chorus of praise and admiration which is raised about her manner and behaviour, and certainly not without justice. It was something very extraordinary and far beyond what was looked for." Melbourne, her first Prime Minister, loved her as a daughter; the Duke of Welling-

ton had a similar feeling for her, which she returned with unstinted confidence and reliance. The first request made by the girl Queen to her mother, immediately after the proclamation, was that she might be left for two hours quite alone to think over her position and strengthen the resolutions that were to guide her future life. The childish words, " I will be good," probably gave the forecast of the tone of the young Queen's reflections. She must have felt the difficulties and peculiar temptations of her position very keenly, for when she was awakened from her sleep on the night of the 20th June 1837, to be told of William the Fourth's death, and that she was Queen of England, her first words to the Archbishop of Canterbury, who made the announcement, were, "I beg your Grace to pray for me."

The Queen was very careful from the beginning of her reign thoroughly to understand all the business of the State, and never to put her signature to any document till she had mastered its contents. Lord Melbourne was heard to declare that this sort of thing was quite new in his experience as Prime Minister, and he said jokingly that he would rather manage ten kings than one Queen. On one occasion he brought a document to her, and urged its importance on the ground of expediency. She looked up quietly, and said, "I have been taught to judge between what is right and what is wrong; but 'expediency' is a word I neither wish to hear nor to understand." Thirty years later one of the best men who ever sat in the House of Commons, John Stuart Mill, said, "There is an important branch of expediency called justice." But this was probably not the kind of expediency that Lord Melbourne recommended, and the Queen condemned.

In the *Memoirs of Mrs. Jameson,* by Mrs. Macphersbn, there is a letter, dated December 1838, containing the following illustration of the way in which the Queen regarded the duties of her position. "Spring Rice told a friend of mine that he once carried her (the Queen) some papers to sign, and said something about managing so as to give Her

Majesty less trouble. She looked up from her paper and said quietly, 'Pray never let me hear those words again; never mention the word "trouble." Only tell me how the thing is to be done, to be done rightly, and I will do it if I can.'" Everything that is known of the Queen at that time shows a similar high conception of duty and right. She was resolved to be no mere pleasureseeking, self-indulgent monarch, but one who strove earnestly to understand her duties, and was determined to throw her best strength into their fulfilment.

It is this conscientious fulfilment of her political duties which gives the Queen such a very strong claim upon the gratitude of all her subjects. People do not always understand how hard and constant her work is, nor how deeply she feels her responsibilities. She is sometimes blamed for not leading society as she did in the earlier years of her reign, and it is no doubt true that her good influence in this way is much missed. Mrs. Oliphant has spoken of the way in which in those early years of her married life she was "in the foreground of the national life, affecting it always for good, and setting an example of purity and virtue. The theatres to which she went, and which both she and her husband enjoyed, were purified by her presence; evils which had been the growth of years disappearing before the face of the young Queen." That good influence at the head of society has been withdrawn by the Queen's withdrawal from fashionable life; and there is another disadvantage arising from her seclusion, in the degree to which it prevents her from feeling the force and value of many of the most important social movements of our time. Except in opening Holloway College, and in the impetus which she has given to providing medical women for the women of India, she has never, for instance, shown any special sympathy with any of the various branches of the movement for improving and lifting up the lives of women. Still, fully allowing all this, it is beyond doubt that her subjects, and especially her women subjects, have deep cause for gratitude and affection to the

Queen. She has set a high example of duty and faithfulness to the whole nation. The childish resolve, "I will be good," has never been lost sight of. With almost boundless opportunities for selfindulgence, and living in an atmosphere where she is necessarily almost entirely removed from the wholesome criticism of equals and friends, she has clung tenaciously to the ideal with which she started on her more than fifty years of sovereignty. Simplicity of daily life and daily hard work are the antidotes which she has constantly applied to counteract the unwholesome influences associated with royalty. Women have special cause for gratitude to her, because she has shown, as no other woman could, how absurd is the statement that political duties unsex a woman, and make her lose womanly tenderness and sympathy. The passionate worship which she bestowed upon her husband, the deep love she constantly shows for her children and grandchildren, and the eager sympathy which she extends to every creature on whom the load of suffering or sorrow has fallen, prove that being the first political officer of the greatest empire in the world cannot harden her heart or dull her sympathy. A woman's a woman "for a' that. "

So much has lately been written about the supreme happiness of the Queen's married life, and so much has been revealed of her inner family circle, that no more is needed to make every woman realise the anguish of the great bereavement of her life. In earlier and happier years she wrote to her uncle Leopold on the occasion of one of the Prince Consort's short absences from her: "You cannot think how much this costs me, nor how completely forlorn I am and feel when he is away, or how I count the hours till he returns. All the numerous children are as nothing to me when he is away. It seems as if the whole life of the house and home were gone." Poor Queen, poor woman! Surely it is ungenerous, while she so strenuously goes on working at the duties of her position, to blame her because she cannot again join in what are supposed

to be its pleasures.

One of the princesses lately spoke of the loneliness of the Queen. "You can have no idea," she is reported to have said, "how lonely mamma is." All who were her elders, and in a sense her guardians and protectors in the earlier part of her reign, have been removed by death. Her strongest affections are in the past, and with the dead. She is reported to have said on the death of one of those nearest to her: "There is no one left to call me Victoria now!" The etiquette which, in public at any rate, rules the behaviour of her children and grandchildren to the Queen, seems to render her isolation more painful than it would otherwise be. Lady Lyttelton, who was governess to the royal children, is stated in the *Greville Memoirs* to have said that "the Queen was very fond of them, but severe in her manner, and a strict disciplinarian." This may have perhaps increased her present loneliness, if it created a sense of reserve and formality between her children and herself.

The Queen has always shown a truly royal appreciation of those who were great in art, science, or literature. It is well known that she sent her book, *Leaves from our Journal in tlie Highlands,* to Charles Dickens, with the inscription, "From one of the humblest of writers to one of the greatest." Mrs. Somerville, in her *Reminiscences,* speaks of the gracious reception given to herself by the Queen while she was still Princess Victoria, when the authoress presented a copy of her *Mechanism of the Heavens* to the Duchess of Kent and her daughter. More than twenty years later Mrs. Somerville wrote, "I am glad to hear that the Queen has been so kind to my friend Faraday. It seems she has given him an apartment at Hampton Court, nicely fitted up. She went to see it herself, and having consulted scientific men as to the instruments necessary for his pursuits, she had a laboratory fitted up with them, and made him a present of the whole. That is doing things handsomely, and no one since Newton has deserved so much." The Queen was also very ready to show her warm appreciation of Carlyle and other eminent writers. In an interview with Carlyle, at the Deanery, Westminster, she quite charmed the rugged old philosopher by her kind and gracious manner. Many years ago, when the fame of Jenny Lind was at its height, she was invited to sing in private before the Queen at Buckingham Palace. Owing to some contemptible spite or jealousy, her accompanist did not play what was set down in the music, and this of course had a very discomposing effect upon the singer. The Queen's quick ear immediately detected what was going on, and at the conclusion of the song, when another was about to be commenced, she stepped up to the piano and said, "I will accompany Miss Lind."

The Queen's strong personal interest in all that concerns the welfare of her kingdom is well known. She became almost ill with anxiety about the sufferings of our troops in the Crimea, and she wrote frequently to Lord Raglan on the subject. Before the end of the siege of Sebastopol, Lord Cardigan returned from the Crimea on a short visit to England, and came to see the Queen at Windsor. One of the royal children said to him, "You must hurry back to Sebastopol and take it, else it will kill mamma!" In the summer of 1886, during the anxious political crisis of that time, a gentleman, who had just seen the Queen, was asked how she looked. "Ten years younger than she did a fortnight ago," was the reply. The severity of the crisis was for the time averted, and the relief of mind it brought to the Queen could be plainly read in the change in her aspect.

A wise and good clergyman, who was also a witty and powerful writer, the Rev. Sydney Smith, preached a sermon in St. Paul's Cathedral on the Queen's accession, in which he gave utterance to the hope that she would promote the spread of national education, and would "worship God by loving peace." "The young Queen," he said, "at that period of life which is commonly given up to frivolous amusement, sees at once the great principles by which she should be guided, and steps at once

into the great duties of her station." He then spoke again of peace and of education as the two objects towards which a patriot Queen ought most earnestly to strive, and concluded: "And then this youthful monarch, profoundly but wisely religious, disdaining hypocrisy, and far above the childish follies of false piety, casts herself upon God, and seeks from the Gospel of His blessed Son a path for her steps and a comfort for her soul. Here is a picture which warms every English heart and could bring all this congregation upon their bended knees before Almighty God to pray it may be realised. What limits to the glory and happiness of our native land, if the Creator should in His mercy have placed in the heart of this Royal Woman the rudiments of wisdom and mercy; and if giving them time to expand, and to bless our children's children with her goodness, He should grant to her a long sojourning on earth, and leave her to reign over us till she is well stricken in years! What glory! what happiness! what joy! what bounty of God!"

The preacher's anticipations of a long reign have been fulfilled, and the bright hopes of that seedtime of promise and resolution can now be compared with the harvest of achievement and fulfilment. There is always a great gap between such anticipations and the accomplished fact; but it will be well for us all, high or low, if we are able, when we stand near the end of life and review the past, to feel that we have been equally steadfast to the high resolves of our youth, as the Queen has been to the words, "I will be good," which she uttered sixty years ago.

vn HARKIET MARTINEAU

Harriet Martineau is one of the most distinguished literary women this century has produced. She is among the few women who have succeeded in the craft of journalism, and one of the still smaller number who succeeded for a time in moulding and shaping the current politics of her day. There are many things in her career which make it a particularly instructive one. Her vivid remembrance of her own childhood gave her a very strong sympathy with the feelings and

sufferings of children; all mothers, especially the mothers of uncommonly intellectual children, ought to read, in the early part of Harriet Martineau's autobiography, her record of her own childhood, and its peculiar sufferings.

The Martineaus were descended from a French Huguenot surgeon, who left his native country in 1688, after the revocation of the edict of Nantes. He settled at Norwich, and became the progenitor of a long line of distinguished surgeons in that city. Harriet's father was a manufacturer; she was born on the 12th June 1802, the sixth of eight children. There is nothing in the outward circumstances of her youth to distinguish it from that of the substantial but simple comfort of any middle class family of that period, save that her education was above the average. The independence of judgment in religious matters that had made their ancestor a Huguenot, made the latter Martineaus Unitarians; and it was to this fact that the excellence of the education of the family was in part due. For the Rev. Isaac Perry, the head of a large and flourishing boys' school in Norwich, became converted to the principles of Unitarianism, with the consequence of losing nearly all his pupils. The Unitarian community felt it their duty to rally round him, and support him to the utmost of their power. Hence those who, like the Martineaus, had children to educate sent them, girls as well as boys, to him. Harriet therefore had the inestimable advantage of beginning her career with a mind well equipped with stores of knowledge that were at that time usually considered quite outside the range of what was necessary for a woman.

She speaks of herself as having, especially in her childhood, "a beggarly nervous system"; and her description of her utterly unreasonable terrors, which she bore in silence, because of the want of insight and sympathy around her, ought to be a lesson to every parent. "Sometimes," she says, "I was panic-struck at the head of the stairs, and was sure I could never get down; and I could never cross the yard into the garden without flying and panting, and fearing to look behind, because a wild beast was after me. The starlight sky was the worst; it was always coming down to stifle and crush me, and rest upon my head." "The extremest terror of all," she says, was occasioned by the dull thud of beating feather beds with a stick, a process in which the housewives of Norwich were wont to indulge on the breezy area below the Castle Hill. A magic-lantern, or the prismatic lights cast by glass lustres upon the wall, threw her into the same unaccountable terror-stricken state. If she could have been coaxed into speaking of these panics, they might probably have ceased to assail her. But this she never dreamed of doing. There was too little tenderness in her family life to overcome her natural timidity. Once when her terror at a magic-lantern so far overcame her as to find vent in a shriek of dismay, "a pretty lady, who sat next us, took me on her lap, and let me hide my face in her bosom, and held me fast. How intensely I loved her, without at all knowing who she was."

When Harriet Martineau was more than fifty, she wrote a detailed account of all she had suffered in childhood, not from any want of gratitude or affection to her parents, but because she felt that mothers ought to know what their children sometimes suffer, so that they might protect them by tender watchfulness from becoming victims of these imaginary terrors. It is not, it must be remembered, stupid children who are most subject to these "ghostly enemies," but much more frequently it is the children of vivid imagination and bright intelligence who are most subject to them. A child who is frightened of the dark ought not to be unkindly ridiculed or forced to endure what terrifies it; it ought to be helped by all gentle means to overcome its fear, and all other unreasonable fears conjured up by its imagination.

That Harriet Martineau showed in early childhood that she was gifted with extraordinary mental powers cannot be doubted At seven years old she "discovered" *Parar dise Lost.* She had been left at home one Sunday evening, when all the rest of the family had gone to chapel, and she began looking at the books on the table. One of them was turned down open. She took it up, and began looking at it It was *Paradise Lost.* The first thing she saw was the word "Argument" at the head of a chapter, which she thought must mean a dispute, and could make nothing of; but something about Satan cleaving Chaos made her turn to the poetry, and, in her own words, that evening's reading fixed her mental destiny for the next seven years; the volume was henceforth never to be found, but by asking her for it. "In a few months, I believe there was hardly a line in *Paradise Lost* that I could not have instantly turned to. I sent myself to sleep by repeating it, and when my curtains were drawn back in the morning, descriptions of heaveidy light rushed into my memory." Her keen appreciation of Milton's great poem was the compensation nature provided for the imaginative terrors which made her childhood such a sad one.

Another misfortune was in store for her, which might have embittered the whole of her future existence. When she was about twelve years old it was recognised that her hearing was not good; by sixteen her deafness had become very noticeable, and excessively painful to herself; and before she was twenty she had become extremely deaf, so that she could hear little or nothing without the help of a trumpet. Few people can realise how much the loss of this all-important sense must have cost her. At the outset of life, to be deprived of a faculty on which almost all free and pleasant social intercourse depends must be a bitter trial. One striking characteristic of Harriet Martineau's mind was brought into relief by it. Throughout her life a misfortune never overtook her without calling out the strength necessary to bear it, not only with patience, but with cheerfulness. As soon as it was clear that her deafness was a trial that would last as long as her life, she made a resolution with regard to it. She determined never to inquire what was said, but to trust to her friends to repeat to her what was important and worth hearing. This she rightly regarded as the only way of preventing her deafness becoming as irksome and trying to her companions as it was to herself. It was not till she was nearly thirty that she began to use a trumpet, and she blamed herself seriously for the delay; for she felt it to be the duty of the deaf to spare other people as much fatigue as possible, and also to preserve their own natural capacity for sound, and the habit of receiving it, as long as possible.

Harriet's first attempt at authorship was undertaken at the age of nineteen; she was tenderly devoted to her brother James, who was two years her junior. When he left home for college, the brightness of her life departed; he told her she must not permit herself to be so miserable, and advised her to take refuge, each time he left her, in some new pursuit; her first new pursuit was writing, and with a beating heart she posted her manuscript to the Editor of the *Monthly Repository,* a Unitarian magazine of that day. She adopted the signature of "V. of Norwich"; all authors will sympathise with what she felt when her manuscript was accepted, and she saw herself for the first time in print. She had not told any member of her family of her enterprise. Imagine therefore her delight when her eldest brother, whom she regarded with the utmost veneration, selected this article by V. of Norwich for special commendation, reading passages from it aloud, and calling upon Harriet to say whether she did not think it first-rate. After a brief attempt to keep her secret, she blurted out, "I never could baffle anybody. The truth is, that paper is mine." The kind brother read on in silence, and as she was going he laid his hand on her shoulder and said gravely (calling her "dear" for the first time), "Now, dear, leave it to other women.to make shirts and darn stockings; and do you devote yourself to this. " "I went home," she adds, "in a sort of dream, so that the squares of the pavement seemed to float before my eyes. That evening made me an authoress."

The trials of her life, however, shortly after this time began to thicken round her. Her beloved elder brother, whose advice had so greatly encouraged her, died of consumption. Her father's business declined rapidly in prosperity; it was a period of great commercial depression, and for a time absolute ruin seemed to stare the family in the face. The cares and the mental strain of this time brought the father to his grave; he died in 1826, when Harriet was twenty-four years of age, leaving his family in comparatively straitened circumstances. Shortly after this Harriet became engaged to be married; but this, instead of bringing happiness, was a source of special trial; for shortly after the engagement had been entered into, her lover became suddenly insane, and after months of severe illness, bodily and mental, he died. The next misfortune was the loss, in 1829, by the mother and daughters of the Martineau family, of nearly all they had in the world. The old manufactory, in which their money had been placed, failed. The way in which she treated this event is very characteristic. "I call it," she wrote, "a misfortune, because in common parlance it would be so treated; but I believe that my mother and all her other daughters would have joined heartily, if asked, in my conviction that it was one of the best things that ever happened to us.... We never recovered more than the merest pittance.... The effect upon me of this new 'calamity,' as people called it, was like that of a blister upon a dull, weary pain or series of pains. / *rather enjoyed it, even at the time;* for there was scope for action, whereas in the long, dreary series of preceding trials, there was nothing possible but endurance. In a very short time my two sisters at home and I began to feel the blessings of a wholly new freedom. I, who had been obliged to write before breakfast, or in some private way, had henceforth liberty to do my own work in my own way; for we had lost our gentility. Many and many a time have we said that, but for the loss of that money, we might have lived on in the ordinary provincial method of ladies with small means, sewing and economising, and growing narrower every year; whereas by being thrown, while it was yet time, on our

own resources, we have worked hard and usefully, won friends, reputation, and independence, seen the world abundantly, abroad and at home, and, in short, have truly lived instead of vegetated" *(Autobiography,* pp. 141, 142).

For a time, notwithstanding the kind brother's advice to Harriet, to leave sewing to other women and devote herself to literature, pressure was brought upon her to get her living by needlework instead of by her pen. She tried to follow both the advice of her friends and her own inclinations. By day she pored over fine needlework, by night she studied and wrote till two or three o'clock in the morning. Instead of being crushed by the double strain, her spirit rose victorious over it. "It was truly *life* I lived during those days," she wrote, "of strong, intellectual, and moral effort. " And again: "Yet I was very happy; the deep-felt sense of progress and expansion was delightful; and so was the exertion of all my faculties, and, not least, that of 'will to overcome any obstructions, and force my way to that power of public speech of which I believed myself more or less worthy." Her first marked literary success was the winning of each of three prizes which had been offered by the Unitarian body for essays presenting the arguments in favour of Unitarianism to the notice of Catholics, Jews, and Mohammedans.

She took every precaution to prevent the discovery that her three essays were by the same hand; and great was the sensation caused by the discovery that this was indeed the case. The most important result to herself of this achievement was that it finally silenced those who wished her to believe that she was fit to do nothing more difficult in the world than bead-work and embroidery. It also set her up in funds to the extent of £45, and she immediately began to plan the work which brought her fame—a series of tales illustrating the most important doctrines of political economy, such as the effect of machinery on wages, the relation of wages and population, free trade, protective duties, and so on. The difficulties she encountered, before she could induce any publisher

to accept her series, were such as would have broken any spirit less heroic and determined than her own/ "I knew the work wanted doing," she said, "and thatT could do it"; and this confidence prevented her from losing heart when one rebuff after another fell upon her. Almost every publisher to whom she applied repeated the cry that the public would attend to nothing at that time (1831) but the cholera and the Reform Bill. She says she became as sick of the Reform Bill as poor King William himself. At length, after a most exhausting and, to any one else, heart-breaking succession of disappointments, her series was accepted, but on terms that made her success in finding a publisher very little pleasure to her. The first stipulation was that 500 copies of the work must be subscribed for before publication, and the agreement was to cease if a thousand copies did not sell in the first fortnight. The dismal business of obtaining subscribers to an unknown work by an unknown author nearly broke her down. But in her darkest hour, alone in London, without money or friends, leaning over some dirty palings, really to recover from an attack of giddiness, but pretending to look at a cabbage bed, she said to herself, as she stood with closed eyes, "My book will do yet."

The day of publication came at last, and Harriet, who had now rejoined her mother in Norwich, eagerly awaited the result. For about ten days she heard nothing, and she began to prepare herself to bear the disappointment of failure. Then at last a letter came, desiring her to make any corrections necessary for a second edition, as the publisher had hardly any copies left. He proposed, he said, to print an additional 2000. A postscript altered the number to 3000, a second postscript suggested 4000, and a third 5000! Her first feeling was that all her cares were now over. Whatever she had to say would now command a hearing, and her anxiety in future would be limited to making a good choice what to write about. Her series made a remarkable sensation; she was overwhelmed with praise from all quarters. Every one who had a hobby wanted her to write a tale to illustrate its importance. Advantageous offers from publishers poured in upon her. Lord Brougham, who was then the leading spirit of the Diffusion of Knowledge Society, declared that the whole Society had been "driven out of the field by a little deaf woman at Norwich."

It soon became evident, from the amount of political and literary work which was pressed upon her, that it was necessary for her to live in London. She accordingly took a small house in Fludyer Street, Westminster, in 1832, where she lived for seven years with her mother and aunt. No change could be greater than that from the provincial society in which she had been brought up, to that into which she was now welcomed. The best of London literary and political society was freely offered her. Cabinet ministers consulted her about their measures, and she enjoyed the acquaintance or friendship of all the foremost men and women of the day. But her head was not turned, and she was not spoiled. Sydney Smith said he had watched her anxiously for one season, and he then declared her unspoilable. The well-founded self-confidence that had made her say to herself, when almost any one else would have despaired, "My book will do yet," prevented her from being dazzled by flattery and social distinction. She knew perfectly well what she could do and what she could not do. It made her angry to hear herself spoken of as a woman of genius; and in correcting a series of errors that had been made in an account given of her personal history in *Men of the Time,* she drily remarks, "Nobody has witnessed 'flashes of wit' from me. The giving me credit for wit shows that the writer is wholly unacquainted with me."

She was a woman of the utmost determination and endurance in carrying out anything she had made up her mind to be right. She once remarked that she had thought the worst that could befall her would be to die of starvation on a doorstep, and added gleefully, "I think I could bear it." Her courage was put rather unexpectedly to the test in 1835,

when she visited the United States. As every one is aware, negro slavery was lawful all over the United States until the civil war of 1862. But every one does not know that the heroic little band of men and women who first protested against the wickedness of slavery in America did so at the peril of their lives. The abolitionists, as they were called, were the objects, even in cities like Boston, usually considered the centres of culture and refinement, of most brutal outrage and cruelty. The abolitionists could not then even hold a meeting but at the peril of their lives. Miss Martineau found herself therefore in a society divided into two hostile factions—one rich, strong, and numerous; the other poor, small, and intensely hated. When she arrived she was disposed to be rather prejudiced against the abolitionists. She condemned slavery as a matter of course, but she thought those who had under

F taken the battle against it in America had been fanatical, sentimental, and misguided. This disposition of her mind was diligently fostered by the defenders of slavery, who represented the abolitionists to her as bloodthirsty ruffians who were trying to incite the slaves to the murder of their masters.

It was not long before her clear intellect discerned the true bearings of the case. She soon acknowledged that, however distasteful to her might be the language used by the abolitionists, they were completely innocent of the charges made against them, and were, in fact, the blameless apostles of a most holy cause. From the time of forming this judgment, her course was clear. She boldly avowed abolitionist principles, and took an early opportunity of attending an anti-slavery meeting at which, in a short speech, she avowed her conviction that slavery was inconsistent with the law of God, and incompatible with the course of His providence. It is unnecessary at this distance of time to recount in detail the fury with which this declaration was regarded by the bulk of American society, and by almost the whole American press. Insult and contumely now met her at every turn, in

quarters where she had before received nothing but adulation and flattery. But she was not of a nature to be induced by threats of personal violence to consent to that which her reason and conscience condemned. She remained then and always an ardent abolitionist, and when the great question of the existence of slavery in the United States was submitted to the arbitrament of war, she was one of the chief among the leaders of political opinion in England who kept our country as a nation free from the guilt and folly of supporting the secession of the Southern States from the American Union. The late Mr. W. E. Forster said at the time that it seemed to him as if Harriet Martineau alone were keeping this country straight in regard to America.

After her return from America she resumed for a time her usual life of work and social activity in London. In a few years, however, her health broke down, and she removed to Tynemouth, suffering, as was then thought, from an incurable disorder. For five years (1837-42) she lay on her couch a helpless, but by no means an idle, invalid. Some of her best books, including her delightful stories for children, *Feats in the Fiord, The Crofton Boys,* etc., were written during this period. She was under the care of a medical brother-in-law, who resided at Newcastle, and some of the most leading of London physicians visited her professionally. But her case was considered chronic, and she resigned herself to the belief that her health was gone for ever. After five years some one persuaded her to try the effects of mesmerism, and some members of her family and many of her former friends were very angry with her for getting well through its means. Her remarks on the subject are characteristic. "For my part," she writes, "if any friend of mine had been lying in a suffering and hopeless state for nearly six years, and if she had fancied she might get well by standing on her head instead of her heels, or reciting charms, or bestriding a broomstick, I should have helped her to try; and thus was I aided by some of my family and by a further sympathy in others, but two or three of them were induced to regard my experiment and recovery as an unpardonable offence, and by them I never was pardoned."

After her recovery she plunged again as heartily as ever into the enjoyment of travel and of work, and finally settled in a little home, which she built for herself, in the Lake country at Ambleside. Here she continued her literary activity, writing her *History of the Peace,* her version of Auguste Comte's philosophy, and at one time contributing as many as six articles a week to the *Daily News.* But she was not content with merely literary labour; she exerted herself most effectually to set on foot, for the benefit of her poorer neighbours, all kinds of means for improving their social, moral, and intellectual position. She showed them, by example, how a farm of two acres could be made to pay. She started a building society, a mechanics' institute, and evening lectures for the people. She was almost worshipped by her servants and immediate dependents, and was a powerful influence for good on all around her. On all moral questions, and all questions affecting the position of women, she was a tower of strength upon the right side. She heartily sympathised with Mrs. Butler in the work with which her name is identified. "I am told," she said, "that this is discreditable work for women, especially for an *old* woman. But it has always been esteemed our special function as women to mount guard over society and social life—the spring of national existence—and to keep them pure; and who so fit as an *old* woman?"

In 1854 it was discovered that she had a heart complaint, which might have been fatal at any moment, but her life was prolonged for more than twenty years after this, closing at Ambleside on 27th June 1876. The words of her friend, Florence Nightingale, might have served as her epitaph—"She served the Right, that is, God, all her life." VIII FLORENCE NIGHTINGALE

Among the personal influences that have altered the everyday life of the present century, the future historian will probably allot a prominent place to that of Florence Nightingale. Before she took up the work of her life, the art of sick nursing in England can hardly have been said to exist. Almost every one had a well-founded horror of the hired nurse; she was often ignorant, cruel, rapacious, and drunken; and when she was not quite as bad as that, she was prejudiced, superstitious, and impervious to new ideas or knowledge. The worst type of the nurse of the pre-Nightingale era has been portrayed by Dickens in his "Sairey Gamp" with her bottle of gin or rum upon the "chimbley piece," handy for her to put it to her lips when she was "so disposged." "Sairey Gamp" is one of the blessings of the good old days which have now vanished for ever; with her disappearance has also gradually disappeared the repugnance with which the professional nurse was at one time almost universally regarded; and there is now hardly any one who has not had cause to be thankful for the quick, gentle, and skilful assistance of the trained nurse whose existence we owe to the example and precepts of Florence Nightingale.

Miss Nightingale has never favoured the curiosity of those who would wish to pry into the details of her private history. She has indeed been so retiring that there is some difficulty in getting accurate information about anything concerning her, with the exception of her public work In a letter she has allowed to be published, she says, "Being naturally a very shy person, most of my life has been distasteful to me." It would be very ungrateful and unbecoming in those who have benefited by her self-forgetful labours to attempt in any way to thwart her desire for privacy as to her personal affairs. The attention of the readers of this sketch will therefore be directed to Miss Nightingale's public work, and what the world, and women in particular, have gained by the noble example she has set of how women's work should be done.

From time immemorial it has been universally recognised that the care of the sick is women's work; but somehow, partly from the low standard of women's education, partly from the false notion that all paid work was in a way degrading to a woman's gentility, it seemed to be imagined that women could do this work of caring for the sick without any special teaching or preparation for it; and as all paid work was supposed to be unladylike, no woman undertook it unless she was driven to it by the dire stress of poverty, and had therefore neither the time nor means to acquire the training necessary to do it well. The lesson of Florence Nightingale's life is that painstaking study and preparation are just as necessary for women's work as they are for men's work. No young man attempts responsible work as a doctor, a lawyer, an engineer, or even a gardener or mechanic, without spending long years in fitting himself for his work; but in old times women seemed to think they could do all their work, in governessing, nursing, or what not, by the light of nature, and without any special teaching and preparation whatever. There is still some temptation on the part of women to fall into this fatal error. A young woman, not long ago, who had studied medicine in India only two years, was placed at the head of a dispensary and hospital for native women. Who would have dreamt of taking a boy, after only two years' study, for a post of similar responsibility and difficulty? Of course failure and disappointment resulted, and it will probably be a long time before the native community in that part of India recover their confidence in lady doctors.

Miss Nightingale spent nearly ten years in studying nursing before she considered herself qualified to undertake the sanitary direction of even a small hospital. She, went from place to place, not confining her studies to her own country. She spent about a year at the hospital and nursing institution at Kaiserswerth on the Rhine in 1849. This had been founded by Pastor Fliedner, and was under the care of a Protestant Sisterhood who had perfected the art of sick nursing to a degree unknown at that time in any other part of Europe. From Kaiserswerth she visited institutions for similar purposes, in other parts of Germany, and in France and Italy. It is obvious she could not have devoted the time and money which all this preparation must have cost if she had not been a member of a wealthy family. The fact that she was so makes her example all the more valuable. She was the daughter and co-heiress of a wealthy country gentleman of Lea Hurst in Derbyshire, and Embly Park in Hampshire. As a young girl she had the choice of all that wealth, luxury, and fashion could offer in the way of self-indulgence and ease, and she set them all on one side for the sake of learning how to benefit suffering humanity by making sick nursing an art in England. In the letter already quoted Miss Nightingale gives, in reply to a special appeal, advice to young women about their work: "1. I would say also to all young ladies who are called to any particular vocation, qualify yourselves for it, as a man does for his work. Don't think you can undertake it otherwise. No one should attempt to teach the Greek language until he is master of the language; and this he can only become by hard studj 2. If you are called to man's work, do not exact a woman's privileges—the privilege of inaccuracy, of weakness, ye muddleheads. Submit yourselves to the rules of business, as men do, by which alone you can make God's business succeed; for He has never said that He will give His success and His blessing to inefficiency, to sketchy and unfinished work"

Here, without intending it, Miss Nightingale drew a picture of her own character and methods. Years of hard study prepared her for her work; no inaccuracy, no weakness, no muddleheadedness was to be found in what she undertook; everything was business-like, orderly, and thorough. Those who knew her in the hospital spoke of her as combining " the voice of velvet and the will of steel." She was not content with having a natural vocation for her work. It is said that when she was a young girl she was accustomed to dress the wounds of those who were hurt in the lead mines and quarries of her Derbyshire home, and that the saying was, "Our good young miss is better than nurse or doctor." If this is accurate, she did not err

by burying her talent in the earth, and thinking that because she had a natural gift there was no need to cultivate it. She saw rather that *because* she had a natural gift it was her duty to increase it and make it of the utmost benefit to mankind. At the end of her ten years' training, she came to the nursing home and hospital for governesses in Harley Street, an excellent institution, which at that time had fallen into some disorder through mismanagement. She stayed here from August 1853 till October 1854, and in those fourteen months placed the domestic, financial, and sanitary affairs of the little hospital on a sound footing.

Now, however, the work with which her name will always be associated, and for which she will always be loved and honoured, was about to commence. The Crimean war broke out early in 1854, and within a very few weeks of the commencement of actual fighting, every one at home was horrified and ashamed to hear of the frightful disorganisation of the supplies, and of the utter breakdown of the commissariat and medical arrangements. The most hopeless hugger-mugger reigned triumphant. The tinned meats sent out from England were little better than poison; ships arrived with stores of boots which proved all to be for the left foot. (Muddleheads do not all belong to one sex.) The medical arrangements for the sick and wounded were on a par with the rest. Mr. Justin M'Carthy, in his *History of Our Own Times,* speaks of the hospitals for the sick and wounded at Scutari as being in an absolutely chaotic condition. "In some instances," he writes, "medical stores were left to decay at Varna, or were found lying useless in the holds of vessels in Balaklava Bay, which were needed for the wounded at Scutari. The medical officers were able and zealous men; the stores were provided and paid for so far as our Government was concerned; but the stores were not brought to the medical men. These had their hands all but idle, their eyes and souls tortured by the sight of sufferings which they were unable to relieve for want of the commonest appli-

ances of the hospital" (vol. ii. p. 316). The result was that the most frightful mortality prevailed, not so much from the inevitable risks of battle, but from the insanitary conditions of the camp, the want of proper food, clothing, and fuel, and the wretched hospital arrangements. Mr. Mackenzie, author of a *History of the Nineteenth Century,* gives the following facts and figures with regard to our total losses in the Crimea: "Out of a total loss of 20,656, only 2598 were slain in battle; 18,058 died in hospital." "Several regiments became literally extinct. One had but seven men left fit for duty; another had thirty. When the sick were put on board transports, to be conveyed to hospital, the mortality was shocking. In some ships one man in every four died in a voyage of seven days. In some of the hospitals recovery was the rare exception. At one time four-fifths of the poor fellows who underwent amputation died of hospital gangrene. During the first seven months of the siege the men perished by disease at a rate which would have extinguished the entire force in little more than a year and a half" (p. 171). When these facts became known in England, the mingled grief, shame, and anger of the whole nation were unbounded. It was then that Mr. Sidney Herbert, who was Minister of War, appealed to Miss Nightingale to organise and take out with her a band of trained nurses. It is needless to say that she consented. She was armed with full authority to cut the swathes of red tape that had proved shrouds to so many of our soldiers. On the 21st of October 1854 Miss Nightingale, accompanied by forty-two other ladies, all trained nurses, set sail for the Crimea. They arrived at Constantinople on 4th November, the eve of Inkerman, which was fought on 5 th November. Their first work, therefore, was to receive into the wards, which were already filled by 2300 men, the wounded from what proved the severest and fiercest engagement of the campaign. Miss Nightingale and her band of nurses proved fully equal to the charge they had undertaken. She, by a combination of inexorable firmness with unvarying gentleness, evolved order out of chaos. After her arrival, there were no more complaints of the inefficiency of the hospital arrangements for the army. The extraordinary way in which she spent herself and let herself be spent will never be forgotten. She lias been known to stand for twenty hours at a stretch, in order to see the wounded provided with every means of easing their condition. Her attention was directed not only to nursing the sick and wounded, but to removing the causes which had made the camp and the hospitals so deadly to their inmates. The extent of the work of mere nursing may be estimated by the fact that a few months after her arrival ten thousand sick men were under her care, and the rows of beds in one hospital alone, the Barrack Hospital at Scutari, measured two miles and one-third in length, with an average distance between each bed of two feet six inches. Miss Nightingale's personal influence and authority over the men were immensely and deservedly strong. They knew she had left the comforts and refinements of a wealthy home to be of service to them. Her slight delicate form, her steady nerve, her kindly conciliating manner, and her absolute self-devotion, awoke a passion of chivalrous feeling on the part of the men she tended. Sometimes a soldier would refuse to submit to a painful but necessary operation until a few calm sentences of hers seemed at once to allay the storm, and the man would submit willingly to the ordeal he had to undergo. One soldier said, "Before she came here, there was such cursin' and swearing, and after that it was as holy as a church." Another said to Mr. Sidney Herbert, "She would speak to one and another, and nod and smile to many more; but she could not do it to all, you know—we lay there in hundreds— but we could kiss her shadow as it fell, and lay our heads on the pillow again, content." This incident, of the wounded soldier turning to kiss her shadow as it passed, has been woven into a beautiful poem by Longfellow. It is called "Santa Filomena." The fact that she had been born in, and had been named after, the city of Florence, may have suggested to

the poet to turn her name into the language of the country of her birth.

Miss Nightingale suffered from an attack of hospital fever in the spring of 1855, but as soon as possible she returned to her laborious post, and never quitted it till the war was over and the last of our soldiers was on his way home. When she returned to England she received such a welcome as probably has fallen to no other woman; all distinctions of party and of rank were forgotten in the one wish to do her honour. She was presented by the Queen with a jewel in commemoration of her work in the Crimea, and a national testimonial was set on foot, to which a sum of £50,000 was subscribed. It is unnecessary to say that Miss Nightingale did not accept this testimonial for her own personal benefit. The sum was devoted to the permanent endowment of schools for the training of nurses in St. Thomas's and King's College Hospitals.

Since the Crimea no European war has taken place without calling forth the service of trained bands of skilled nurses. Within ten years of Florence Nightingale's labours in the East, the nations of Europe agreed at the Geneva Convention upon certain rules and regulations, with the object of ameliorating the condition of the sick and wounded in war. By this convention all ambulances and military hospitals were neutralised, and their inmates and staff were henceforth to be regarded as non-combatants. The distinguishing red cross of the Geneva Convention is now universally recognised as the one civilised element in the savagery of war.

During a great part of the years that have passed since Miss Nightingale returned from the Crimea, she has suffered from extremely bad health; but few people, even of the most robust frame, have done better and more invaluable work. She has been the adviser of successive Governments on the sanitary condition of the army in India; her experience in the Crimea convinced her that the death-rate in the army, even in time of peace, could be reduced by nearly one-half by proper sanitary

arrangements. She contributed valuable state papers on the subject to the Government of the day, and her advice has had important effects, not only on the condition of the army, but also on the sanitary reform of many of the towns of India, and on the extension of irrigation in that country. Besides this department of useful public work, she has written many books on the subjects she has made particularly her own; among them may be mentioned *Notes on Hospitals* and *Notes on Nursing;* the latter in particular is a book which no family ought to be without.

It will surprise no one to hear that she is very zealous for all that can lift up and improve the lives of women, and give them a higher conception of their duties and responsibilities. She supports the extension of parliamentary representation to women, generally, however, putting in a word in what she writes on the subject, to remind people that representatives will never be better than the people they represent. Therefore the most important thing for men, as well as for women, is to improve the education and morality of the elector, and then Parliament will improve itself. Every honest effort for the good of men or women has her sympathy, and a large number her generous support. May she long be spared to the country she has served so well, a living example of strength, courage, and self-forgetfulness—

A noble type of good
Heroic womanhood.
SANTA FILOMENA.
BY H. W. LONGFELLOW.
Whene'er a noble deed is wrought,
Whene'er is spoken a noble thought.
    Our hearts, in glad surprise,
    To higher levels rise.
    The tidal wave of deeper souls
Into our inmost being rolls,
    And lifts us unawares
    Out of all meaner cares.
    Honour to those whose words or deeds
Thus help us in our daily needs,
    And by their overflow
    Raise us from what is low.
    Thus thought I, as by night I read

Of the great army of the dead,
The trenches cold and damp,
The starved and frozen camp.
　The wounded from the battle plain
In dreary hospitals of pain,
　The cheerless corridors,
　The cold and stony floors.
　Lo! in that house of misery
　A lady with a lamp I see
　Pass through the glimmering gloom,
And flit from room to room.
　And slow, as in a dream of bliss,
The speechless sufferer turns to kiss
　Her shadow, as it falls
Upon the darkening walls.
　As if a door in heaven should be
Opened, and then closed suddenly,
The vision came and went,
The light shone and was spent.
　On England's annals, through the long
Hereafter of her speech and song,
That light its rays shall cast
From portals of the past.
　A lady with a lamp shall stand
In the great history of the land,
　A noble type of good
　Heroic womanhood.
　Nor even shall bo wanting here
The palm, the lily, and the spear,
　The symbols that of yore
　Saint Filomena bore.

MARY LAMB

The name of Mary Lamb can never be mentioned without recalling that of her brother Charles, and the devoted, self-sacrificing love that existed between the two. It was one of Harriet Martineau's sayings, that of all relations that between brother and sister was apt to be the least satisfactory. There have been some notable examples to the contrary, and perhaps the most notable is that given by Charles and Mary Lamb. When a brother and sister are linked together by an unusually strong bond of affection and admiration, it is generally the sister who, by inclination and natural selection, sacrifices all individual and personal objects for the sake of the brother. For instance, she frequently remains unmarried in order to be able to devote herself to his pursuits and further his interests. There is no more devotedly unselfish love than that of a sister and

brother when it is at its best. The love of a wife for a husband, or a parent for a child, has something in it more of the element of self. In both these relationships, the husband and wife and the parent and child are so closely and indissolubly identified with one another that it is comparatively easy to merge the love between them into self-love. But between a brother and sister this is not the case. The bond that unites the two ca.n be set aside by either of them at will. It is partly voluntary in its character, and, as previously remarked, in the give and take of this affection, it is, speaking generally, the brother who takes and the sister who gives. The contrary, however, was the case with Charles and Mary Lamb. Between these two, it was the brother who laid down his life for his sister, sacrificing for her sake, at the outset of his own career, his prospects of love and marriage, the ease and comfort of his life, and his opportunities of devoting himself exclusively to his darling studies.

The story of these two beautiful lives is worth more than even their contributions to English literature, and makes us love Lamb and his sister quite independently of the *Essays of Elm,* and the *Tales from Shakespeare.* Mary Lamb was born in 1764, eleven years before her brother Charles. Her childhood, till the birth of this precious brother, seems to have had little brightness in it. There was a tendency to insanity in the Lamb family, and this tendency was probably intensified in Mary's case by the harshness and want of sympathy with which it was then the fashion to treat children. "Polly, what are those poor crazy, moythered brains of yours thinking, always *l"* was a speech of her grandmother's that made a lasting impression on the sensitive child. The love of her parents, her mother especially, seems to have been centred on her brother John, older than herself by two years. "'Dear little selfish, craving John,' he was in childhood, and dear big selfish John he remained in manhood" (Mrs. Gilchrist's *Life of Mary Lamb,* p. 4).

The first creature upon whom the wealth of affection in Mary's nature

could be freely bestowed was, therefore, the baby brother. She spoke in after years of the curative influence on her mind of the almost maternal affection which she lavished on the boy who was, to a great extent, committed to her care. Henceforward she was no longer lonely, but had gained a companion and object in life. Her education consisted mainly in having been "tumbled early, by accident or design, into a spacious closet of good old English reading, without much selection or prohibition, and she browsed at will upon that fair and wholesome pasturage." This was the library of Mr. Salt, a bencher of the Inner Temple, to whom her father was clerk. In 1782, when Charles was seven and Mary eighteen, he became a scholar of the Blue Coat School, where he formed a lifelong friendship with the poet Coleridge. The circumstances of the Lambs gradually narrowed. The father was superannuated, and his income was consequently reduced. The elder brother, John, held a good appointment in the South Sea House, but he was much more intent on enjoying himself and surrounding himself with luxuries than upon providing for the wants of his family. For eleven years, from the age of twenty-one to thirty-two, Mary supported herself by her needle.

The father's mental faculties gradually gave way more and more. By the time Charles was fifteen he left school, and the care and maintenance of his family in a short time devolved mainly on him. He first obtained a clerkship in the same establishment where his brother was employed, and two years later he received a better paid appointment, with a salary of £70 a year, in the India House. Domestic troubles, however, thickened upon the family; the mother became a confirmed invalid, and in 1795 Charles was seized by an attack of the madness hereditary in the family. This affliction must have weighed terribly upon Mary, who thus saw her one prop and solace taken from her. She was left alone, with her father in his second childhood, her mother an exacting and imperious invalid, and an old Aunt Hetty, who was for ever poring over devotional books, without apparently the capacity of sharing any of the household burdens. No sooner was Charles restored to reason than a new trouble began. John met with a serious accident, and, though in his days of prosperity his family saw little or nothing of him, he now returned home to be nursed. This seems to have been the last straw that broke poor Mary down. In September 1796 the mania, with which she had been

G often threatened, broke out; she seized a knife from the table and stabbed her mother to the heart. The poor old father was almost unconscious of what had taken place; Aunt Hetty fainted. It was Charles who seized the knife from his sister's grasp, but not before she had, in her frenzy, inflicted a slight wound on her father. The horror of the whole scene can be with difficulty pictured. Yet Charles, who had only lately been released from an asylum, had the power to cope with it, to maintain his calmness and courage, and above all to resolve that the terrible calamity which had overtaken them should not be allowed to enshroud the whole of his dear sister's life in the gloom of a madhouse. He wrote to his friend Coleridge five days after the tragedy, and his letter speaks nothing but tender fortitude. "God has preserved to me my senses," he writes. "I eat, and drink, and sleep, and have my judgment, I believe, very sound. My poor father was slightly wounded, and I am left to take care of him and of my aunt.... With me 'the former things are passed away,' and I have something more to do than to feel."

Severe self-mastery is perceived in every word of this letter. Lamb was evidently sensible that his own reason would totter if it were not controlled by a strong effort of will. In another letter written a week later to the same friend, the same spirit is shown; he had already formed the determination not to allow his sister to remain in a madhouse; he resolved to devote his life to her, and to give up all thought of other happiness for himself than what was consistent with his being her constant companion

and guardian—" Your letter was an inestimable treasure to me. It will be a comfort to you, I know, to know that my prospects are somewhat brighter. My poor dear, dearest sister—the unhappy and unconscious instrument of the Almighty's judgments on our house— is restored to her senses, to a dreadful sense and recollection of what has past, awful to her mind, and impressive (as it must be to the end of life), but tempered with religious resignation and the reasonings of a sound judgment, which in this early stage knows how to distinguish between a deed committed in a transient fit of frenzy and the terrible guilt of a mother's murder. I have seen her. I found her this morning calm and serene, far, very far, from an indecent, forgetful serenity; she has a most affectionate and tender concern for what has happened. Indeed from the beginning, frightful and hopeless as her disorder seemed, I had confidence enough in her strength of mind and religious principle to look forward to a time when *even she* might recover tranquillity. God be praised, Coleridge, wonderful as it is to tell, I have never once been otherwise than collected and calm; even on the dreadful day, and in the midst of the terrible scene, I preserved a tranquillity which bystanders may have construed into indifference—a tranquillity not of despair. Is it folly or sin in me to say that it was a religious principle that most supported me?... I felt I had something else to do than to regret. On that first evening, my aunt was lying insensible, to all appearance like one dying, — my father with his poor forehead plastered over from a wound he had received from a daughter dearly loved by him, who loved him no less dearly,— my mother, a dead and murdered corpse in the next room,—yet was I wonderfully supported. I closed not my eyes that night, but lay without terrors and without despair. I have lost no sleep since. I had been long used not to rest in things of sense, had endeavoured after a comprehension of mind unsatisfied with the ignorant present time; and this kept me up. I had the whole weight of the family thrown on me, for my brother, little dis-

posed (I speak not without tenderness for him) at any time to take care of old age and infirmities, had now, with his bad leg, an exemption from such duties; and I was now left alone." He then speaks of the kindness of various friends, and reckons up the resources of the family, resolving to spare £50 or £60 a year to keep Mary at a private asylum at Islington. "I know John will make speeches about it, but she shall not go into an hospital.... If my father, and old maid-servant, and I, can't live, and live comfortably, on £130 or £120 a year, we ought to burn by slow fires; and I almost would, that Mary might not go into an hospital. Let me not leave an unfavourable impression on your mind respecting my brother. Since this has happened, he has been very kind and brotherly, but I fear for his mind. He has taken his ease in the world, and is not fit to struggle with difficulties, nor has much accustomed himself to throw himself into their way; and I know his language is already, 'Charles, you must take care of yourself, you must not abridge yourself of a single pleasure you have been used to,' etc.; and in that style of talking." Charles goes *on* to explain that his sister would form one of the family she had been placed with rather than a patient. "They, as the saying is, take to her extraordinarily, if it is extraordinary that people who see my sister should love her. Of all the people I ever saw in the world, my poor sister was most thoroughly devoid of the quality of selfishness. I will enlarge upon her qualities, dearest soul, in a future letter for my own comfort, for I understand her thoroughly; and if I mistake not, in the most trying situation that a human being can be found in, she will be found... uniformly great and amiable. God keep her in her present mind, to whom be thanks and praise for all His dispensations to mankind."

The whole of the rest of Lamb's life was a fulfilment of the loving resolutions which had sustained him in the terrible hour of his mother's death. His love for the beautiful Alice W n was relinquished as one of the

"tender fond records" for ever blotted

out by a sterner, more imperative claim of affection and duty. As soon as the old father died, Mary and Charles were reunited in one home, and her brother's guardianship was accepted by the authorities as a sufficient guarantee that any future return of her malady should not be accompanied by danger to the lives of others. He was faithful to his selfimposed task. He himself was never again attacked by the cruel malady, but his sister to the end of her life was subject to recurring periods of insanity, which latterly isolated her from her friends for months in every year. Through their joint care and caution no fatal results again attended these attacks of. mania. There is something inexpressibly touching in the fact that on their holiday excursions together, Mary invariably, with her own hands, packed a strait-waistcoat for herself. She was able to foretell, by premonitory symptoms, when she was likely to be attacked; and a friend of the Lambs has related how he had met them walking together, hand in hand, towards the asylum, both weeping bitterly.

Lamb's strong feeling against allowing his sister to be placed in an hospital for lunatics is more than justified by the accounts given, in the *Life of Lord Shaftesbury,* of the frightfully barbarous treatment to which insane people were subjected in the early part of the present century. Their keepers always visited them whip in hand. They were sometimes spun round on rotatory chairs at a tremendous speed; sometimes they were chained in wells, in which the water was made to rise till it reached their chins; sometimes they were left quite alone, chained to their beds, from Saturday afternoon to Monday morning, unable to rise, and with nothing but bread and water within their-reach. No wonder that Charles Lamb said he would burn by slow fires rather than let his sister be treated like this.

The strong restorative of work done and duty fulfilled enabled Charles, within little more than a year of the dreadful calamity which had darkened his life, to make his first appearance as an author. These first poems were ded-

icated to "the author's best friend and sister." He wished to fence her round, as it were, by assurances of the high value he set on her, and of the depth of his love. "I wish," he wrote to Coleridge, "to accumulate perpetuating tokens of my affection to poor Mary." When she was restored to his daily companionship, there was nothing in her outward manner or appearance to indicate what a terrible cloud rested on her past life. Her manners were tranquil and composed. De Quincey speaks of her as that "Madonna-like lady." There was no appearance of settled melancholy in consequence of the fatal deed she" had been led to commit, but that it left a wound which was hidden rather than healed is indicated by the words written long years after the event: "My dear mother who, though you do not know it, is always in my poor head and heart." On another occasion, a child Mary loved asked her why she never spoke of her mother. A cry of pain was the only response. Her dependence on her brother was an ever-visible presence in both their lives. Mrs. Cowden Clarke relates: "He once said, with his peculiar mode of tenderness beneath blunt, abrupt speech, 'You must die first, Mary.' She nodded, with her little quiet nod and sweet smile, 'Yes, I must die first, Charles.'" The event was contrary to the wish and expectation thus expressed. Charles preceded Mary to the grave by thirteen years; but during the greater part of that time her intellect was so clouded as to deprive her of the power of the acute suffering the loss of her brother would otherwise have caused.

The literary fame of Mary Lamb rests chiefly on her *Tales from Shakespeare,* and a collection of beautiful little stories for children, called *Mrs. Leicester's School.* The *Tales from Shakespeare* were written, as so much good work has been, under the stress of poverty. Six of the great tragedies were undertaken by Charles, and fourteen other plays by Mary. The scheme was to render each play into a prose story fit for the comprehension and capacity of children; and the work was done with inimitable felicity of diction, and critical insight

into the situations and characters of the world of men and women who live in Shakespeare's dramas. There is a letter of Mary's describing herself and Charles at work: "Charles has written *Macbeth, Othello, King Lear,* and has begun *Hamlet.* You would like to see us, as we often sit writing on one table (but not on one cushion sitting, like Hermia and Helena in the *Midsummer Nights Dream);* or rather, like an old literary Darby and Joan, I taking snuff, and he groaning all the while and saying he can make nothing of it, which he always says till he has finished, and then he finds out that he has made something of it" (Mrs. Gilchrist's *Life,* p. 119). The *Tales* were written for William Godwin, whose first wife was Mary Wollstonecraft. His second wife helped him a great deal with his publishing business. She was a vulgar-minded woman, and a pet aversion of the Lambs, especially of Charles, who said, referring to her, "I will be buried with this inscription over me, 'Here lies C. L., the woman-hater' —I mean, that hated one woman; for the rest, God bless 'em." The success of the *Tales* could not, however, be marred by the unpopularity of the publisher and his wife. The book rapidly ran through several editions, and even now a year seldom passes without the *Tales from Shakespeare* being presented to the public in some new form.

A portrait of Mary Lamb has been drawn by the master hand of her brother. She is the Bridget of the *Essays of Elia,* as all lovers of the essays well know. The humour and delicate insight into character for which the writings of Charles Lamb are so distinguished, are also characteristic of Mary, though the humour in her case is less rollicking, and never breaks out in pure high spirits, as his often does. Some of the most charming of Mary's writings are her letters, which have been published in Mrs. Gilchrist's *Life,* especially those to a young friend, named Sarah Stoddart.

This young lady had a most "business-like determination to marry "; and as she generally had more than one string to her bow, as the saying is, it is no wonder that she sometimes needed the help of an older and wiser woman than herself, to get her out of the difficulties in which she found herself. Much of Mary's own character comes out in the advice she gives her friend. She speaks in one place of her power of valuing people for what they are, without demanding or expecting perfection. It is a "knack I know I have, of looking into people's real character, and never expecting them to act out of it— never expecting another to do as I would in the same case." How much practical wisdom there is in this, and what misunderstandings and heart-burnings would be saved if it were more common not to expect people to act out of their own characters! There is a funny little bit in another letter to the effect that women should not be constantly admonishing men as to the right line of thought and conduct. "I make it a point of conscience never to interfere or cross my brother in the humour he happens to be ia It always appears to me a vexatious kind of tyranny, that women have no business to exercise over men, which merely because, *they having a better judgment,* they have power to do. Let *men* alone, and at last we find they come round to the right way which *we,* by a kind of intuition, perceive at once. But better, far better, that we should let them often do wrong than that they should have the torment of a monitor always at their elbows."

To begin quoting from the letters of Charles and Mary Lamb is such an enticing task that it would be easy to fill more pages than this little book contains. One more only shall be quoted from each. The most beautiful of Mary's letters is perhaps that which she wrote to Dorothy Wordsworth, soon after the death by drowning of Wordsworth's brother John. The beautiful poem by Wordsworth, "The Happy Warrior," is supposed to have been written partly in reference to this brother, and partly in reference to Nelson, whose death took place the same year (1805). "I thank you," Mary wrote, "my kind friend, for your most comfortable letter; till I saw your own handwriting I could not persuade myself that I should do

well to write to you, though I have often attempted it.... I wished to tell you that you would one day feel the kind of peaceful state of mind and sweet memory of the dead which you so happily describe as now almost begun; but I felt that it was improper, and most grating to the feelings of the afflicted, to say to them that the memory of their affliction would in time become a constant part, not only of their dream, but of their most wakeful sense of happiness. That you would see every object with, and through, your lost brother, and that that would at last become a real and everlasting source of comfort to you, I felt and well knew from my own experience in sorrow; but till you yourself began to feel this I didn't dare tell you so."

How terrible that the mind and heart which could dictate such words as these were weighed down-by the lifelong burden of insanity! Before Miss Wordsworth's reply reached her, she was again attacked, and Charles wrote in her place: "I have every reason to suppose that this illness, like all the former ones, will be but temporary; but I cannot always feel so. Meantime she is dead to me, and I miss a prop. All my strength is gone, and I am like a fool, bereft of her co-operation. I dare not think, lest I should think wrong, so used am I to look up to her in the least as in the biggest perplexity. To say all that I know of her would be more than I think anybody could believe, or even understand; and when I hope to have her well again with me, it would be sinning against her feelings to go about praising her, for I can conceal nothing that I do from her. She is older and wiser and better than I, and all my wretched imperfections I cover to myself by resolutely thinking on her goodness. She would share life and death, heaven and hell, with me. She lives but for me; and I know I have been wasting and teasing her life for five years past incessantly, with my cursed drinking and ways of going on. But even in thus upbraiding myself I am offending against her, for I know that she has clung to me for better, for worse; and if the balance has been against her hitherto it was a noble trade.

"

Great, noble spirits they both were, even in their weaknesses and imperfections, showing an example of devoted unselfishness, tenderness, and generosity that many who "tithe mint and anise and cummin" might envy. Mary Lamb survived to old age, dying in May 1847, aged seventy-three. She was buried by her brother's side in the churchyard at Edmonton.

AGNES ELIZABETH JONES

"Count not that man's life short who has had time to do noble deeds."— From Cicero.

There is something very interesting in tracing, as we are sometimes able to do, the connection of one piece of good work with another. The energy, devotion, and success of one worker stimulates the enthusiasm of others; this enthusiasm does not always show itself in carrying on or developing what has been already begun, but sometimes manifests itself in the more difficult task of breaking new ground; and thus one good work becomes the parent of another. An example of what is here referred to is to be found in the work of Mrs. Fry. To her initiative may be traced not only the kindred labours of Mary Carpenter in reformatory and industrial schools, and the still more modern efforts for the better care of neglected children by the boarding-out system, and by such societies as the Metropolitan Association for Befriending Young Servants, but to her also may indirectly be traced the success with which women have devoted themselves to the art of sick nursing, and from this again has spread or grown out the movement for extending to women a thorough medical education and training.

Mrs. Fry's connection with the art of sick nursing came about in this way. In the first quarter of this century a young German named Fliedner was appointed pastor to the little weaving village of Kaiserswerth on the Rhine. He endeared himself to his people by his devotion to them; but the time came when he was forced to leave them. The whole village was involved in ruin because of the failure of the industry on which its inhabitants depended. The people not only could not support their pastor, but were themselves reduced to the greatest straits of actual want. He left them in order to seek in wealthier places, not maintenance for himself, but help for them. After travelling for some time in Germany, he came to England, and while here, still intent on making known the wants of Kaiserswerth, he met with Mrs. Fry, and was deeply interested in all she was doing for the benefit of prisoners. Not long after this he returned to Kaiserswerth, bearing with him the gifts he had collected to relieve the pressing wants of his people; but his mind was now full of Mrs. Fry, and of what was being done in England by and for women. He and his wife resolved to begin similar work in Germany. They began with two young women just discharged from a neighbouring prison, whose relations refused to receive them or have anything further to do with them. Soon the number of discharged prisoners increased, and the pastor and his wife felt that they must have help; a friend therefore came to join them in their work. In this way and from this small beginning grew in time a very large institution, comprising not only an organisation to enable discharged prisoners to get work and regain their character, but a home and school for orphans, a hospital for the sick, and an asylum for lunatics. The whole of the work of this institution, which occupied several houses and comprised more than 300 persons, was done by carefully-trained women, called deaconesses.

Kaiserswerth was the parent of all the other deaconesses' institutions which now exist in almost every part of the world. The predominating spirit at Kaiserswerth, after that of religious self-devotion, to which a first place was given, was that the work of caring for the poor, the sick, and the afflicted can only be rightly undertaken after a long course of special preparation and training. It was a Protestant sisterhood; those who entered were first called novices; in time the novices became deaconesses, and the deaconesses were expected to bind themselves to remain in the institution five years. They were, however, bound by no vows, and could always leave if other duties seemed to require that they should do so. In this institution the art of sick nursing acquired a perfection at that time unknown in any other part of Europe. It was here, mainly, that Florence Nightingale received the training which enabled her to save the lives of so many of our soldiers in the Crimea, and to introduce into England a new era in the history of nursing. Here too Agnes Elizabeth Jones was trained.

Miss Nightingale's often-repeated lesson on the subject of the necessity of long and careful training was not lost upon Agnes Jones. When she left Kaiserswerth, she knew, as Miss Nightingale said, "more than most hospital matrons know when they undertake matronship." But she was not content with this. After working for a time with the London Bible Women's Mission, she applied to the training-school for nurses at St. Thomas's Hospital for another year's training. She entered the hospital as a "Nightingale probationer." She went through, while she was there, the whole training of a nurse. To quote Miss Nightingale again, referring to this period, "Her reports of cases were admirable as to nursing details. She was our best pupil; *she went through all the work of a soldier, and she thereby fitted herself for being the best general we ever had.*"

Before referring to Agnes Jones's crowning work in reorganising the nursing staff of the Liverpool Workhouse Infirmary, it will be well to recall the story of her life. There are few incidents in it, none at all of a sensational character; but perhaps this makes the lesson to be learnt from it all the more plain and simple.

She was born at Cambridge, of Irish parents, in 1832. Her father was a colonel in the 12th Regiment, and her descent was from the north Irish stock that has furnished so many great names to the roll-call of the worthies of our nation. She was a Protestant evangelical, of the type which northern Ireland produces. It is easy to label the religious sect to which she belonged as narrow and unattractive; but however this may be, as exemplified in her personally, her religion was too intense a reality to be unattractive. It permeated her whole life, from the time when as a child of seven her dream was to become a missionary, to the hour when she died of typhus taken from a patient in the Liverpool Infirmary to whom she had given up her own room and bed. Another deep and permanent influence on her mind and character was her love for Ireland. Over and over again in her letters we come across expressions which show how close to her heart lay her country's good. The training at Kaiserswerth was intended to be utilised for the good of Ireland. "I have no desire," she wrote, "to become a deaconess; that would not, I think, be the place I should be called upon to occupy. No, my own Ireland first. It was for Ireland's good that my first desire to be used as a blessed instrument in God's hand was breathed,... . and in Ireland is it my heart's desire to labour...."

In another letter she refers to the time when she "then and there" dedicated herself to do what she could for Ireland, in its workhouses, infirmaries, and hospitals. In another place she speaks of being retained in England for another year's training, and exclaims, "My last English sojourn, I hope, as Ireland is ever my bourn!" And again, "My heart is ever in Ireland, where I hope ultimately to work." Her heart's desire was never gratified; she laid down her life, at the age of thirty-five, in the Liverpool Workhouse, before she had had an opportunity of giving to her own dear land the benefit of all she had learned by the patient years of training at Kaiserswerth and in London. Ulster Protestant as she was to the backbone, and a member of the Church of England, she was a true patriot, and showed her patriotism by labouring with self-denying earnestness to fit herself to lift up to a higher level an important branch of the social life of her country.

She was very much stimulated, as so many women were, by the heroism of the Nightingale band of nurses who left England for the Crimea in 1854. She listened with vehement inward dissent to those who cast contempt and blame on them, and, in her own words, "almost worshipped" their brave leader.

She had paid a visit of a week to Kaiserswerth in 1853, but home duties, especially the care of a widowed sister, at that time and for some years prevented her from fulfilling her strong desire for a course of thorough training in the art of nursing. It was not till 1860 that she returned to Kaiserswerth for this purpose. Very soon after her year of preparation there, she received, through Miss Nightingale, an invitation from Mr. W. Rathbone to undertake the superintendence of the Liverpool Training School for Nurses of the Poor. She was overwhelmed by a genuine sense of her inadequacy to the task. She was a sincerely humble-minded woman, and not only craved more training in the mechanical difficulties of nursing, but doubted her own powers of organising, directing, and superintending. She hesitated, and while hesitating, joined Mrs. Kanyard in her London Biblewoman's Mission. Her work here was interrupted by a telegram summoning her to Rome to nurse a sick sister. As soon as the sister recovered, another invalid relative claimed her. By their bedsides she felt, to a certain extent, her own power, and the question often arose in her mind, "Could I govern and teach others?" As soon as these private cares were over, she visited nursing institutions in Switzerland, France, and Germany, and before she returned to England she determined to go for another year's training to St. Thomas's Hospital, and then to offer herself for the difficult post at Liverpool. "I determined," she writes, "at least to try.... If every one shrinks back because incompetent, who will ever do anything?' Lord, here am I; send me.'"

She did not on leaving St. Thomas's immediately commence her work at Liverpool. She was for a short time superintendent of a small hospital in Bolsover Street, and later she filled a similar post at the Great Northern Hospital. It was not till the spring of 1865 that she took the place at Liver-

pool with which her name is chiefly connected.

The old system in pauper infirmaries was to allow the patients to be "nursed" by old inmates of the workhouse. Among those to whom the care of the sick was confided were "worn-out old thieves, worn-out old drunkards," and worse. Mr. W. Rathbone, of Liverpool, strongly urged on the guardians of that place to do away with this wretched system, and to substitute in the place of these ignorant, and often vicious, women a staff of trained paid nurses. He generously undertook to defray the whole cost of the new scheme for three years, by which time he believed the improvement effected would be so great that no one would for a moment dream of going back to the old plan. It was to the post of superintendent of the band of trained nurses that Agnes Jones was called in the spring of 1865.

It was no light task for a young woman of thirty-three. She had under her about 50 nurses, 150 pauper "scourers," and from 1220 to 1350 patients. The winters of 1865 and 1866 will long be remembered as the terrible period of the cotton famine in Lancashire. The workhouse infirmary at Liverpool was not only full, but overflowing; a number of patients often arrived when every bed was full. Then the gentle authority of Sister Agnes, as she was called, had to be exercised to induce the wild, rough patients to make way for one another. Sometimes she had to persuade them to let her put the beds together and place three or even four in two beds. The children had to be packed together, some at the head and some at the foot of the bed. She speaks of them as "nests of children," and mentions that forty under twelve were sent in in one day. This over-filling of the workhouse was of course no ordinary occurrence, and was due to the exceptional distress in Lancashire at that time. The number of deaths that took place, for the same reason, was unusually large. Sister Agnes speaks in one of her letters of seven deaths having occurred between Sunday night and Tuesday morning.

The dreadful melancholy of the place

bore upon her with terrible weight. There was not only the depressing thought that most of the inmates were there in consequence of their own wickedness or folly, but added to this the patients were isolated from friends and relatives whose visits do so much to cheer an ordinary hospital. There were patients with *delirium tremens* wandering about the wards in their shirts; there were little children, some not more than seven, steeped in every kind of vice and infamy. "I sometimes wonder," she wrote, in a' moment of despair, "if there is a worse place on earth than Liverpool, and I am sure its workhouse is burdened with a large proportion of its vilest."

Some of the best and most deeply-rooted instincts of human nature seemed to turn into cruelty and gall in this terrible place. One of the difficulties of the nurses was to prevent the mothers of the babies, who were still at the breast, from fighting and stealing one another's food. They had nothing to do but nurse their babies, and they would hardly do that. The noise, quarrelling, and dirt prevailing in their neighbourhood was a constant source of trouble and anxiety. Another trouble was the mixture among the patients of criminal cases, necessitating the presence of policemen constantly on the premises. The ex-pauper women, too, whom Sister Agnes was endeavouring to train as assistant nurses, were a great anxiety. One morning, after they had been paid their wages, five arrived at the hospital tipsy; after some months of constant effort and constant disappointment, the attempt to train these women was given up. Besides the strain on nerves, temper, and spirit arising from all these causes, the physical work of Agnes Jones's post was no light matter. Her day began at 5.30 A.M. and ended after 11; added to this, if there was any case about which she was specially anxious, or any

H nurse about whose competence she did not feel fully assured, she would be up two or three times in the night to satisfy herself that all was going well. Her nurses were devoted to her, and, as a rule, gave her no anxiety or discomfort which could be avoided. Her only distress on their account arose from a severe outbreak of fever and small-pox among them, which was a source of much painful anxiety to her. Miss Nightingale said of her that " she had a greater power of carrying her followers with her than any woman (or man) I ever knew." "Her influence with her nurses was unbounded. They would have died for her."

All witnesses concur in speaking of her wonderful personal influence *tmd* the effect it produced. The infirmary began to show the results of her presence within a month of her arrival. In the three years she spent there, she completely changed the whole place. At first the police, to whose presence reference has already been made, were astonished that it was safe for a number of young women to be about in the men's wards, for they well knew what a rough lot some of the patients were; but "in less than three years she had reduced one of the most disorderly hospital populations in the world to something like Christian discipline, such as the police themselves wondered at. She had led, so as to be of one mind and one heart with her, upwards of fifty nurses and probationers.... She had converted a vestry to the conviction of the economy as well as the humanity of nursing pauper sick by trained nurses.... She had converted the Poor Law Board to the same view, and she had disarmed all opposition, all sectarian zealotism; so that Roman Catholic and Unitarian, High Church and Low Church, all literally rose up and called her blessed."

The manner of her death has been already referred to. It was in unison with her unselfish, devoted life. She died on the 19th February 1868, and her body was committed to the earth of her beloved Ireland, at Fahan, on Lough Swilly, the home of her early years.

CHARLOTTE AND EMILY BRONTE

In the quiet Yorkshire village of Haworth, on the bleak moorland hillside above Keighley, were born two of the greatest imaginative writers of the present century, Charlotte and Emily

Bronte. The wonderful gifts of the Bronte family, the grief and tragedy that overshadowed their lives, and their early deaths, will always cast about their story a peculiarly touching interest. Their father, the Rev. Patrick Bronte, was of Irish birth. He was born in the County Down, of a Protestant family— one that had migrated from the south to the north of Ireland. His character was that which we are more accustomed to associate with Scotland than with Ireland. Resolute, stern, independent, and self-denying, he had the virtues of an old Covenanter rather than the facile graces which so often distinguish those of Celtic blood. His father was a farmer, but Patrick Bronte had no desire to live by agricultural industry. At sixteen years of age he separated himself from his family and opened a school. What amount of success he had in this undertaking does not appear, but it is evident that he had a distinct object in view, namely, to obtain money enough to complete his own education; in this he was successful, for after nine years' labour in instructing others, he entered as a student in St. John's College, Cambridge, remained there four years, obtained the B.A. degree of the University, and was ordained as a clergyman of the Church of England. He kept up no intercourse with his family, and showed no trace of his Irish blood, either in speech or character. He loved and married Miss Branwell, of Penzance, a lady of much sweetness and refinement. Their six children were destined, through the writings of two of them, to be known wherever the English language is spoken, all over the world. After holding livings in Essex and at Thornton, in Yorkshire, Mr. Bronte was appointed to the Rectory of Haworth, which is now so often visited on account of its association with the authors of *Jane Eyre* and *Wuihering Heights*.

Mrs. Bronte's six children were born in rapid succession, and her naturally delicate constitution was further tried by the constant labour and anxiety involved in providing, on very limited means, for the wants of the little brood. Mrs. Gaskell, in her *Life of Charlotte*

Bronte, appears to imply that, more than is even usually the case, the weight of family cares and anxieties fell upon the mother rather than the father. "Mr. Bronte," she says, "was, of course, much engaged in his study, and besides, he was not naturally fond of children, and felt their frequent appearance upon the scene as a drag both on his wife's strength and as an interruption to the comfort of the household." One feels disposed to comment on this by saying that children ought never to be born if either of their parents inclines to regard them "as an interruption to the comfort of the household." To give life and grudge it at the same time is not an attractive combination of qualities. Though not much helped-by her husband, Mrs. Bronte was, however, not alone in her domestic cares and duties; the eldest of the "interruptions to the comfort of the household," Maria, was a child of wonderfully precocious intellect and heart. Her remarkable character was described in after years by her sister Charlotte as the Helen Burns of *Jane Eyre*. In her, her mother found a sympathising companion and a helper in her domestic cares. The time was rapidly approaching when the mother's place in the household would be vacant, and when many of its duties and responsibilities would be discharged by Maria.

The little Bronte's were from their birth unlike other children. The room dedicated to their use was not, even in their babyhood, called their nursery; it was their "study." Little Maria at seven years old would shut herself up in this study with the newspaper, and be able to converse with her father on all the public events of the day, and instruct the other children as to current politics, and upon the characters of the chief personages of the political world.

Mrs. Bronte died in 1821. Maria was then eight; Elizabeth, seven; Charlotte, five; Patrick Branwell, four; Emily, three; and Anne, one. The little motherless brood were left alone for a year, when an elder sister of their mother came to live at the parsonage, but she does not seem to have had any real influence over them. She taught the girls to stitch and sew, and to become proficient in various domestic arts, but she had no sympathy or communion with them, and their real life was lived quite apart from hers. As soon almost as they could read and write at all, they began to compose plays and act them; they had no society but each other's; this, however, was all-sufficient for them. Their power of invention and imagination was very marked; to the habit of composing stories in their own minds they gave the name of "making out." As soon as the labour of writing became less formidable than it always is to baby fingers, the stories thus "made out" were written down. In fifteen months, when Charlotte was about twelve to thirteen years of age, she wrote twenty-two volumes of manuscript, in the minutest hand, which can hardly be deciphered except with the aid of a magnifying-glass. The Duke of Wellington filled a large place in the minds of the Brontes, and in their romances. Something of what the hero was to them when they were children, Charlotte afterwards put into the mouth of Shirley, the heroine of her novel of that name. After the manner of imaginative children, she not only worshipped her hero from afar, but identified herself with him or with members of his family. The authorship of many of her childish romances and poems is ascribed, in her imagination, to the Marquis of Douro, or Lord Charles Wellesley; and when these "goodly youths" are not introduced as authors they often become the chief personages of the story.

The shadow of death that casts so deep a gloom over the story of the Bronte family, first fell on Maria and Elizabeth, the two elder children. The four girls—Maria, Elizabeth, Charlotte, and Emily—had been sent to a school, which was partly a charitable institution, at Cowan Bridge, in Westmoreland. The living at Haworth parsonage was the reverse of luxurious, but the food and the sanitary arrangements at Cowan Bridge were so bad that the health of the little Brontes was seriously injured by it. The food was repulsive from the want of cleanliness with which it was prepared and placed on the table.

The children frequently refused food altogether, though sinking from the want of it, rather than drink the "bingy" milk, and eat unappetising scraps from a dirty larder, and puddings made with water taken from rain-tubs and impregnated with the smell of soot and dust. Besides the faulty domestic arrangements of the school, the discipline was harsh and tyrannical, and one teacher in particular was guilty of conduct towards Maria Bronte that can only be called brutal. Low fever broke out at the school, from which about forty of the pupils suffered, but the Brontes did not take the disease. It was evident that Maria was destined for another fate, that of consumption. She was removed from the school only a few days before her death, and Elizabeth followed her to the grave about six weeks later, in June 1825. Even after this Mr. Bronte's eyes were not opened to the danger his children were in by their treatment at Cowan Bridge, and Charlotte and Emily were still allowed to remain at the school. It soon, however, became evident that they would not be long in following Maria and Elizabeth unless they were removed; and they returned home before the rigours of another winter set in. All the physical and mental tortures she endured at Cowan Bridge, Charlotte afterwards described in the account she gives of "Lowood" in Jane Eyre. It is not to be taken that the account of "Lowood" is as strictly an accurate description of Cowan Bridge as Charlotte Bronte would have given if she had been simply writing a history of the school. The facts are, perhaps, magnified by the lurid glow of passion and grief with which she recalled her sisters' sufferings. She was only between nine and ten when she left Cowan Bridge, and in the account she wrote of it twenty years later we see rather the impression that was left on her imagination than a strictly accurate history; but there is no doubt that in her account of Maria Bronte's angelic patience, and the cruel persecution to which she was subjected by one of the teachers, the Lowood of Jane Eyre is a perfectly faithful transcript of what took place at Cowan Bridge. Mrs.

Gaskell says, "Not a word of that part of Jane Eyre but is a literal repetition of scenes between the pupil and the teacher. Those who had been pupils at the same time knew who must have written the book from the force with which Helen Burns's sufferings are described."

After the death of Maria and Elizabeth, the next great sorrow of the Bronte family arose from the career of the only son, Patrick Branwell. He was a handsome boy of exceptional mental powers. He had in particular the gift of brilliant conversation, and there was hardly anything he attempted in the way of talking, writing, or drawing which he did not do well. In one of Charlotte's letters she says, "You ask me if I do not think that men are strange beings / I do, indeed. I have often thought so; and I think, too, that the mode of bringing them up is strange; they are not sufficiently guarded from temptation. Girls are protected as if they were something very frail and silly indeed, while boys are turned loose on the world, as if they of all beings in existence were the wisest and least liable to be led astray." Poor Branwell, with his brilliant social qualities, was not sufficiently guarded from temptation

The easiest outlet from the narrow walls of Haworth parsonage was to be found at the little inn of Haworth village. The habit of the place was, when any stranger arrived at the inn, for the host to send for the brilliant boy from the parsonage to amuse the guest. The result will easily be guessed. The guiding principle of Charlotte's character was her inexorable fidelity to duty; her whole nature turned with irresistible force to what was right rather than to what was pleasant. With Branwell the reverse was the case. Conventional propriety of course strictly guarded Charlotte from the possible dangers of associating with casual strangers at the village inn, although her strong resolute character would not have run a tenth part of the risk of contamination as did that of the weak, pleasure-seeking Branwell. It is needless to dwell on the details of his gradual degradation; the high ideals and hopes of his youth were given up; his character became at once coarse and weak He was entirely incapable of selfgovernment and of retaining any kind of respectable employment. His intemperance and other vices made the daily life of his sisters at the parsonage a nightmare of horrors. For eight years the young man, whose boyhood his family had watched with so much hope and pride, was a source of shame and anguish to them, all the more keenly felt because it could not be openly avowed. Many who knew the family affirmed that so far as purely intellectual qualities were concerned Branwell was even more eminently distinguished than his sisters; but mere intellect, without moral power to guide it, is as dangerous as a spirited horse without bit or bridle. Branwell was singularly deficient in that moral power in which his sisters were so strong, and his education did nothing to supply this natural deficiency. He died in 1848, at the age of thirty.

Cowan Bridge was not the only experience Charlotte and Emily had of school life. They went for a time to another school at Boe Head, where Charlotte was very happy, and in 1835 she returned to the same school as a teacher. In 1842 Charlotte and Emily went to a school in Brussels, where the former stayed two years, the latter only one. All that Charlotte saw and all the friends she made were afterwards portrayed in her stories. One of her most intimate friends became the Caroline Helstone of *Shirley;* the originals of Rose and Jessie Yorke were also among her schoolfellows at Roe Head. There can be little doubt that M. Paul Emanuel of Villette was M. Heger of the Brussels school. Every trivial circumstance of an unusually uneventful life became food for her imagination.

The development of Emily's genius was different. Her love of the moors around Haworth was so intense that it was impossible for her to thrive when she was away from them. It became a fact recognised by all the family that Emily must not be taken away from home. The solitude of the wild, dark moors, and the communing with her own heart, together with the dark tragedy of Branwell's wasted life, were the sole sources of Emily's inspiration. Her poems have a wild, untameable quality in them, and her one romance, *Wuthering Heights,* places her in the first rank among the great imaginative writers of English fiction. There is something terrible in Emily's sternness of character, which she never vented pitilessly on any one but herself. She was deeply reserved, and hardly ever, even to her sisters, spoke of what she felt most intensely. A friend who furnished Mrs. Gaskell with some particulars for her biography, states that on one occasion she mentioned " that some one had asked me what religion I was of (with the view of getting me for a partisan), and that I had said that was between God and me. Emily, who was lying on the hearth-rug, exclaimed, 'That's right.' This was all," adds the friend, "I ever heard Emily say on religious subjects." Emily's love for animals was intense; she was especially devoted to a savage old bull-dog named Keeper, who owned no master but herself. The incident in *Shirley* of the heroine being bitten by a mad dog, and straightway burning the wound herself with a red-hot Italian iron, was true of Emily. Her last illness was a time of terrible agony to Charlotte and Anne, not merely because they saw that she who, Charlotte said, was the thing that seemed nearest to her heart in the world was going to be taken from them, but because Emily's resistance to the inroads of illness was so terrible. She resolutely refused to see a doctor, and she would allow no nursing and no tender helpfulness of any kind. It was evident to her agonised sisters that she was dying, but she maintained her savage reserve, suffering in solitary silence rather than admit her pain and weakness. On the very day of her death she rose as usual, dressed herself, and attempted to cany on her usual employments, and all this with the catching, rattling breath and the glazing eye which told that the hand of Death was actually upon her. Charlotte wrote in this agonising hour,

"Moments so dark as these I have never known. I pray for God's support to us all. Hitherto He has granted it." At noon on that day, when it was too late, Emily whispered in gasps, "If you will send for a doctor, I will see him now." A few days later Charlotte wrote, "We are very calm at present. Why should we be otherwise? The anguish of seeing her suffer is over; the spectacle of the pains of death is gone by; the funeral day is past. We feel she is at peace. No need to tremble for the hard frost and the keen wind. Emily does not feel them." The terrible anguish of those last days haunted the surviving sisters like a vision of doom. Nearly six months later Charlotte wrote again that nothing but hope in the life to come had kept her heart from breaking. "I cannot forget," she says, "Emily's death-day; it becomes a more fixed, a darker, a more frequently recurring idea in my mind than ever. It was very terrible. She was torn, conscious, panting, reluctant, though resolute, out of a happy life." Within a very short time the gentle youngest sister Anne also died, and Charlotte was left with her father, the last survivor of the family of six wonderful children who had come to Haworth twenty-nine years before.

In earlier and happier days the habit of the sisters had been, when their aunt went to bed at nine o'clock, to put out the candles and pace up and down the room discussing the plots of their novels, and making plans and projects for their future life. Now Charlotte was left to pace the room alone, with all that had been dearest to her in the world under the church pavement at Haworth and in the old churchyard at Scarborough. But Charlotte was not one to give way to self-indulgent idleness, even in the hour of darkest despair. She was writing *Shirley* at the time of Anne's last illness. After the death of this beloved and only remaining sister, she resumed her task; but those who knew what her private history at the time was, can trace in the pages of the novel what she had gone through. The first chapter she wrote after the death of Anne is called, "The Valley of the Shadow of Death."

The first venture in authorship of the

sisters was a volume of poems, to which they each contributed. They imagined, probably with justice, that the world was at that time prejudiced against literary women. Therefore they were careful to conceal, even from their publishers, their real identity. The poems were published as the writings of Currer, Ellis, and Acton Bell.

Jane Eyre was the first of Charlotte's stories which was published, but *The Professor* was the first that was written with a view to publication. The sisters each wrote a story—Charlotte, *The Professor;* Emily, *Wuthering Heights;* and Anne, *Agnes Grey,* and sent them to various publishers. Charlotte was the only one of the three sisters whose manuscript was returned on her hands. But she was not discouraged by the disappointment. Just at this time Mr. Bronte, who had been suffering from cataract, was persuaded by his daughters to go to Manchester for an operation. Charlotte accompanied him, and it was while she was waiting on him, in the long suspense after the operation had been performed, that she began *Jane Eyre,* the book that made her, and ultimately the name of Bronte, famous. Nothing is more striking in Charlotte's personal history than the way in which she reproduced the events and personages of her own circle into her novels. Probably the belief that she was writing anonymously encouraged her in this. Her father's threatened blindness and her own fear of a similar calamity are reflected, as it were, in the blindness of Rochester in *Jane Eyre.* The success of *Jane Eyre* was rapid and complete, and there was much dispute whether its author were a man or a woman. The *Quarterly Review* distinguished itself by the remark that if the author were a woman it was evident "she must be one who for some sufficient reason has long forfeited the society of her sex." Sensitive as Charlotte Bronte was, the coarseness of the insult could not wound her; it could at the utmost be regarded as nothing worse than a trivial annoyance; for when the words reached Charlotte, the grave had not long closed over Branwell's wasted life; Emily was just dead, and it was ev-

ident that Anne was dying. The greatness of her grief and the anguish of her loneliness dwarfed to their proper proportions the petty insults that at another time would have caused her acute pain. On the whole she had nothing to complain of in the way her book was received; she suffered no lack of generous appreciation from the real leaders of the literary world. Thackeray and *G. H.* Lewes, Miss Martineau, and Sidney Dobell were warm in their praise of her work. Charlotte's manner of making her literary fame known to her father was characteristic. The secret of their authorship had been very strictly kept by the sisters; but when the success of *Jane Eyre* was assured, Emily and Anne urged Charlotte that their father ought to be allowed to share the pleasure of knowing that she was the writer of the book. Accordingly one afternoon Charlotte entered her father's study and said, "Papa, I've been writing a book." When Mr. Bronte found that the book was not only written, but printed and published, he exclaimed, "My dear, you've never thought of the expense it will be! It will be almost sure to be a loss, for how can you get a book sold? No one knows you or your name."

"But, papa, I don't think it will be a loss; no more will you, if you will just let me read you a review or two, and tell you more about it." At tea that evening Mr Bronte exclaimed to his other daughters, "Girls, do you know that Charlotte has been writing a book, and it is much better than likely?"

The pacing up and down of the sisters in the firelight, discussing the plots of their novels, has been already mentioned. Mrs. Gaskell records that Charlotte told her that these discussions seldom had any effect in causing her to change the events in her stories, "so possessed was she with the feeling that she had described reality." This confirms what Mr. Swinburne has said of her strongest characteristic as an author, that she has the power of making the reader feel in every nerve that thus and not otherwise it must have been. It must not, however, be thought that the conversations with her sisters were there-

fore useless; no doubt they were very stimulating to her imagination, and gave her creations more solid reality than they would otherwise have had.

In 1854 Charlotte Bronte married Mr. Nicholls, an Irish gentleman, who had for eight years been her father's curate. She only lived nine months after her marriage. She was happy in her husband's love, and appreciated his devotion to his parish duties. But the loving admirers of Charlotte Bronte can never feel much enthusiasm for Mr. Nicholls. Mrs. Gaskell states that he was not attracted by her literary fame, but was rather repelled by it; he appears to have used her up remorselessly, in their short married life, in the routine drudgery of parish work. She did not complain; on the contrary, she seemed more than contented to sacrifice everything for him and his work; but she remarks in one of her letters, "I have less time for thinking." Apparently she had none for writing. Surely the husband of a Charlotte Bronte, just as much as the wife of a Wordsworth or a Tennyson, ought to be attracted by literary fame. To be the life partner of one to whom the most precious of Nature's gifts is confided, and to be unappreciative of it and even repelled by it, shows a littleness of nature and essential meanness of soul. A true wife or husband of one of these gifted beings should rather regard herself or himself as responsible to the world for making the conditions of the daily life of their distinguished partners favourable to the development of their genius. But pearls have before now been cast before swine, and one cannot but regret that Charlotte Bronte was married to a man *who* did not value her place in literature as he ought ELIZABETH BARRETT BROWNING

Sydney Smith, writing in 1810 upon the extraordinary folly of closing to women all the ordinary means of literary education, remarked that one consequence of their exclusion was that no woman had contributed anything of lasting value to English, French, or Italian literature, and that scarcely a single woman had crept into the ranks even of the minor poets. While he was writing this, a little baby girl was beginning to prattle, who within a very short time was destined to win a place among the great poets of this century. The very great gifts of Elizabeth Barrett were discernible from her earliest childhood. Her father was Mr. Edward Moulton, of Burn Hall, Durham. The date and place of her birth are disputed. Mrs. Richmond Ritchie states in the *National Dictionary of Biography* that the future poetess was born at Burn Hall, Durham, in 1809; Mr. J. H. Ingram says in his *Life of Mrs. Browning* in the Eminent Women Series that she was born in London in 1809; while Mr. Browning has written to the papers to say that she was born at Carlton Hall, Durham, in 1806. Three birthplaces and two birthdays are thus assigned to her. It is not, however, disputed that she was christened by the names of Elizabeth Barrett, and that her father afterwards exchanged the name of Moulton for that of Barrett on inheriting some property from a relative. At eight years old little Elizabeth could read Homer in the original Greek, and was often to be seen with the *Iliad* in one hand and a doll in the other; this picture of her gives a beautiful type of her future character, its depth of loving womanliness, combined with the height of poetic inspiration and learning. She was certainly one of the women of whom her brother poet, Tennyson, sings, who "gain in mental breadth nor fail in childward care." She says herself of her childhood that "she dreamed more of Agamemnon than of Moses her black pony." At about eleven years old she wrote an epic poem in four books on *The Battle of Marathon,* which her father caused to be printed. Her home, during most of her childhood, was at Hope End, near Ledbury, in Herefordshire. Many pictures of her happy childhood among the beautiful hills and orchards of the West country are to be found in the poems, especially in "Hector in the Garden" and in her "Lost Bower." Much of her young life, too, is described in the earlier part of her greatest work, *Aurora Leigh.* We do not hear much about the mother of the poetess, but her grandmother, it is said,

looked with much disfavour on the little lady's learning, and said she would "rather hear that Elizabeth's hemming were more carefully finished than of all this Greek." Her father, however, was a worthy guardian of the wonderful child that had been entrusted to him; he fostered and encouraged her genius by all means in his power. He must have had a singular power of self-devotion and selfsacrifice; and it is probable that much of his daughter's beautiful moral nature was inherited from him. When Elizabeth was about twenty, her mother lay in her last illness, and simultaneously money troubles, brought on by no fault of his own, fell upon Mr. Barrett. He would allow no knowledge of this to disturb his wife during her illness; and in order effectually to hide the truth from her, he made an arrangement with his creditors which very materially reduced his income for life, so that no reduction of his establishment should take place as long as his wife lived. Two other misfortunes had an important influence on Elizabeth Barrett's youth. When she was about fifteen, she was trying to saddle her pony by herself in the paddock, when she was thrown to the ground, and her spine was injured in a manner that kept her lying on her back for four years. Scarcely had she recovered from this injury, when another terrible calamity nearly overwhelmed her. She had been sent to Torquay for the benefit of her health, and had been there nearly a year, when her eldest brother came to visit her, in order to consult her about some trouble of his own. With two other young men, all good sailors, he took a little boat, intending to have a sail along the coast. Within a few minutes of starting, and almost under his sister's window, the boat went down, and young Barrett and his companions were drowned. The grief and horror caused by this terrible event nearly killed her. It was almost a year before she could be moved by slow stages of twenty miles a day to London. Those who knew her best at that time believe that she would have died if she had not been sustained by her love of literary pursuits, which afforded some relief to

her mind from the constant dwelling on the tragedy of which she accused herself of being the cause. Miss Mitford says in her *Literary Recollections:* "The house she occupied at Torquay had been chosen as one of the most sheltered in the place. It stood at the bottom of the cliffs, almost close to the sea; and she told me herself that during that whole winter the sound of the waves rang in her ears like the moans of one dying. Still she clung to literature and Greek; in all probability she would have died without that wholesome diversion to her thoughts. Her medical attendant did not always understand this. To prevent the remonstrance of her friendly physician, Dr. Barry, she caused a small edition of Plato to be so bound as to resemble a novel. He did not know, skilful and kind though he were, that to her such books were not an arduous and painful study, but a consolation and a delight." She, however, appeared to be condemned to a life of perpetual invalidism. She now lived in London with her father, and was confined to one large darkened room, and saw no one but her own family, and a few intimate friends, the chief of whom were Miss Mitford, Mrs. Jameson, and Mr. John Kenyon. The impression she produced on all who came into contact with her was that she was the most charming and delightful person they had ever met. Her sweetness, her purity, and the tender womanliness of her character, made her friends forget her learning and her genius. Miss Mitford says she often travelled five-and-forty miles expressly to see her, and returned the same evening without entering another house. The seclusion in which she lived was perhaps not unfavourable to literary work. She lay on her couch, not only, as Miss Mitford says, reading every book worth reading in almost every language, but "giving herself heart and soul to that poetry of which she seemed born to be the priestess." In 1835 she published *Prometheus and other Poems,* which, in the opinion of the most competent judges, raised her at once to a high rank among English poets. In 1843 she wrote *The Cry of the Children,* to which Lord Shaftesbury owed so much in his efforts to protect factory children from being ground to death by overwork; and later she wrote the noble "Song for the Bagged Schools of London," whose words go straight to every mother's heart.

During her long period of illness her chief link with the outside world was her cousin, Mr. John Kenyon, to whom *Aurora Leigh* is dedicated. He knew all who were best worth knowing in the great world of London, and he occasionally introduced to her one and another of those whom he believed to be most capable of appreciating her and pleasing her. In this way, in 1846, he brought Mr. Robert Browning to see Miss Barrett. In the autumn of that same year the poet and poetess were married. What his love was for her and hers for him may be gathered in the lovely poem, "Caterina to Camoens," and in the forty-three *Sonnets from the Portuguese,* which Mrs. Browning wrote before her marriage. Almost directly after her marriage Mrs. Browning was ordered abroad for the benefit of her health, and the chief part of the remaining fifteen years of her life was spent in Italy. She identified herself completely with those who were struggling for the unity and independence of Italy, and much of her poetry from this time onwards is coloured by her political convictions. In Florence, in 1849, her only child, Robert Browning the younger, was born. The deep joy of motherhood suffuses much of the noblest part of *Aurora Leigh.* One is tempted to believe that the lovely description of Marian Erie bending over her sleeping child,

The yearling creature, warm and moist with life

To the bottom of his dimples,

could have been written by no one who had not felt a mother's love. In any case, it adds to one's pleasure in reading it to know that the poetess was drawing her inspiration from her own excessive happiness in the bliss of motherhood.

Many have singled out Mrs. Browning's *Sonnets from the Portuguese* as her chief work. Mrs. Ritchie, in a very interesting article in the *National Dictionary of Biography,* says of them,

"There is a quality in them which is beyond words: an echo from afar, which belongs to the highest human expression of feeling." Many other of the best judges have said they are among the greatest sonnets in the English language. But the work for which the world is most deeply in her debt is *Aurora Leigh.* It probes to the bottom, but with a hand guided by purity and justice, those social problems which lie at the root of what are known as women's questions. Her intense feeling that the honour of manhood can never be reached while the honour of womanhood is sullied; her no less profound conviction that people can never be raised to a higher level by mere material prosperity, make this book one of the most precious in our language. She herself speaks of it in the dedication as "The most mature of my works, and the one into which my highest convictions upon Life and Art have entered." If she had written nothing else, she would stand out as one of the epoch-making poets of the present century.

Mr. Browning has published some interesting information as to the manner in which he and his wife worked. They were very careful not to influence each other's compositions unduly. Their styles in writing are entirely unlike. They abstained from reading each other's poems while they were in process of composition. Mrs. Browning always kept a low writing-table, with inkstand and pen upon it, by her side. Mr. Browning wrote: "My wife used to write it *(Aurora Leigh)* and lay it down to hear our child spell, or when a visitor came in it was thrust under the cushions. At Paris, a year ago last March, she gave me the first six books to read, I never having seen a line before. She then wrote the rest and transcribed them in London, where I read them also. I wish, in one sense, that I had written and she had read it." No one but a poet could have expressed so perfectly the great pleasure the reading gave him. There is an anecdote that when the Brownings left Florence for London, in 1856, the box containing the MS. of *Aurora Leigh* was lost at Marseilles. It

also contained the velvet suits and lace collars of the little boy; and it is said that Mrs. Browning was far more distressed at losing the latter than the former. However, both were fortunately recovered, for the box containing them was found by Mrs. Browning's brother in one of the dark recesses of the Marseilles Custom House.

As evidence of her position in the literary world, it may be mentioned that when Wordsworth died in 1850 the *Aihenmum* strongly urged that Mrs. Browning ought to be made Poet Laureate.

Her sympathy with Italy was so strong that it is believed that the news of the death of Cavour, through whom in so large a measure the unity of Italy was achieved, hastened her own. She was very ill when the news reached her, and she died in Florence on 30th June 1861. The municipality of Florence placed a tablet upon her house expressing their gratitude and admiration for her, and saying that in her womanly heart she had reconciled the wisdom of the learned with the enthusiasm of the poet, and with her verses had made a golden ring uniting Italy with England.

XIII LADY SALE AND HER FELLOW-HOSTAGES

IN AFGHANISTAN

The first Napoleon is said to have remarked to Madame de Stael that women had nothing to do with politics; whereupon the lady rejoined that women ought at least to be sufficiently acquainted with political subjects to understand the reason why their heads were cut off. When we read the account of the great sufferings of the English ladies who were held as prisoners or hostages by Akbar Khan in Afghanistan in 1842, we are reminded of Madame de Stael's epigram, and think that they ought at least to have had the consolation of understanding the political meddling and muddling, which led to the prolonged pain and danger to which they were subjected.

Afghanistan is a wild mountainous country beyond the north-west frontier of the British Empire in India. Its people consist of savage, desperate, lawless tribes, constantly at war with one another; indeed, they are hardly ever united unless they are attacked by some foreign foe. They are particularly jealous of any kind of foreign influence or interference. Every man among them is bred to arms, even children being provided with dangerous knives; they are trained to great endurance, they are splendid horsemen, and are proficient in many kinds of manly sports and martial exercises; but with these superficially attractive qualities they possess others of a different stamp, for they are treacherous, utterly regardless of truth, revengeful, bloodthirsty, sensual, and avaricious. It will thus be seen that both their good and their bad qualities render them particularly dangerous as foes. The character of their country is very much like their own. It is a land of rocky mountain passes, and a great part of it is savage and sterile. It is separated from India by narrow rocky defiles, the principal one of which, the Khyber pass, is twenty-eight miles long, and runs between lofty, almost perpendicular precipices; the pass itself is so covered with rocks and boulders that progress along it, even under the most favourable circumstances, must necessarily be very slow. The rocky precipices which command the pass are so steep that they cannot be mounted; but they are perforated by many natural caves, which for centuries have been the strongholds of bands of robbers. It is easy to understand that an army endeavouring to go through this pass is at a terrible disadvantage, and is almost entirely at the mercy of the wild tribes of warriors and robbers who infest the heights.

About 1838-39 there was more than usual of internal fighting between the savage tribes of Afghanistan. Some tribes wished for Dost Mahomed as their king, or Ameer, and others wished for Shaj Soojah. It was considered by those who directed the policy of the British Government in India, a favourable time for us to interfere. It appears to have been thought that we should make the ruler of Afghanistan our friend, if he felt that he owed his throne to our espousal of his cause. It was, however,

forgotten that, however much the Afghans quarrelled among themselves, they would forget all past enmities and unite against a foreigner who tried to intervene between them; and they would hate and despise any ruler who owed his nominal sovereignty to the help of foreign soldiers. Therefore, although the English succeeded, in the first instance, in driving away Dost Mahomed and making Shaj Soojah king, they soon found that this first success was the beginning of their difficulties. Sir George Lawrence has told the story in his interesting book called *Forty-three Years of my Life in India,* and another narrative of the same events may be found in *Lady Sale's Journal.* An Afghan horseman, with whom Sir George (then Major) Lawrence conversed, expressed the feelings of his countrymen and the difficulties of our position in a few words. ""What could induce you," he said, "to squander crores of rupees in coming to a poor rocky country like ours, without wood or water, and all in order to force upon us a kumbukbt (unlucky person) as a king, who, the moment you turn your backs, will be upset by Dost Mahomed, our *own* king?"

However, for a time the English army in Afghanistan did not realise the difficult and dangerous position in which they were placed. Dost Mahomed fled; and not long after he surrendered himself to the English, and was sent, with his wives and children, as a prisoner of war to India. Everybody now thought all trouble and danger were over, and the married officers and men of the English garrison sent for their wives and children to join them at Cabul. Shaj Soojah was established there and received the congratulations of the English. Lawrence, however, observed that the Ameer's own subjects did not join in these congratulations, and moreover Shaj Soojah himself began to show signs of getting tired of his English friends. No special danger was, however, anticipated; the English envoy, Sir W. MacNaghten, was about to leave Cabul, having been appointed to the Governorship of Bombay. Had he left, he would have taken Lawrence with

him as his secretary. When the preparations for his departure were nearly complete, the clouds that had long been gathering at last burst in storm. The Ghilzye tribe rose in rebellion because they had been deprived of an annual subsidy of £3000, nominally paid them by Shaj Soojah, but really supplied by the British. This insurrection had the effect of a match applied to a train of gunpowder.

A crore of rupees is a million. At that time a rupee was worth 2s.; therefore a crore of rupees would equal £100,000. The whole of Afghanistan was presently in arms; the safest and most easily defended routes for the return to India were cut off. The insurrection spread to Cabul itself; the houses of the English residents were attacked and burned, the Treasury was sacked, and several officers and men were murdered in the streets. An attempt to send help to the English from Jellalabad was unsuccessful; the Afghans were victorious, and held the small British force entirely in their power.

Sir George Lawrence and Lady Sale complain bitterly of the incapacity of those who were highest in command of the English military operations; they urged that the right thing to have done would have been to take the whole British force into the Bala Hissar, the citadel of Cabul, and hold it against all comers till reinforcements arrived. The time of year was mid-winter, and winter in Afghanistan is intensely severe. To have held the fort would have entailed far less difficulty and danger than to attempt to retreat by the fearful Khyber pass, the heights of which were held by bands of savage mountaineers. This rash and fatal course was, however, attempted, with the result, now well known, that of the whole army, with the exception of those who were held by the Afghans as prisoners or hostages, only one man, and he severely wounded, reached Jellalabad alive. Those who have seen Lady Butler's picture, "The Last of an Army," will be able to realise something of what the disaster of the Khyber pass was. Akbar Khan, a son of Dost Mahomed and the leading spirit of the Afghan chiefs, had said that he would destroy the army with the exception of one man who should be left to tell the tale, and he kept his word.

Before this fatal retreat was decided upon, attempts at negotiation with the Afghans were made; Akbar, in particular, had repeatedly demanded that, as a pledge of good faith, the wives and children of the English officers and men should be delivered over to him as hostages. While the English were still in Cabul, this suggestion was naturally rejected with horror. Some officers declared they would rather shoot their wives with their own hands than put them in the power of Akbar. Akbar had shown himself desperately cruel and treacherous. He twice invited the English envoy, Sir W. MacNaghten, outside the encampment to consult with him and other chiefs as to the terms of capitulation. On the first occasion the envoy and his escort returned in safety, but the terms of the treaty agreed upon were, on the part of the Afghans, entirely set at naught. When the second conference was about to take place, the English were treacherously attacked and overpowered, and our envoy was murdered by Akbar with his own hands. It was not very likely therefore that the repeated demand of this man to have the English women and children placed in his control would be listened to, and it was not, in fact, conceded until it became evident that to continue to accompany the ill-fated army in its retreat meant certain death.

The retreat from Cabul began on the 6th January 1842; the.thermometer was ten degrees below zero—far colder than the coldest weather of an ordinary English winter. The night was spent in the open; part of the march had been through snow and slush, which wetted those on foot up to their knees. Lady Sale, who was riding, says her habit was like a sheet of ice. Many died of cold and exhaustion on the first night. The poor Sepoys, accustomed to the warmth of an Indian sun, were unable to handle their muskets, and when attacked by the murderous bands of Afghans that continually pursued the army, were cut

down as helplessly as sheep. The sufferings of the women and children were terrible. One poor woman had lately been confined. She, as well as the others, was exposed to all the horrors of the Afghan winter, and to the chances of dying by the Afghan knife or bullet. Lady Sale, with her daughter Mrs. Sturt, showed a fine example of courage and endurance. Lawrence said she and all the ladies bore up so nobly and heroically against hunger, cold, and fatigue, as to call forth the admiration even of the Afghans themselves. It seems to have been known or rumoured that Akbar would make a special effort to get hold of the women, for Lady Sale and her daughter were advised to disguise themselves as much as possible, and to ride with the men, which they did, riding with Captain Hay's troopers. On the second day of the retreat they were heavily fired upon, Lady Sale was wounded, her daughter's horse was shot under her, and her son-in-law, Captain Sturt, was mortally injured. Let any one who likes to dwell on " the pomp and circumstance of glorious war" look on the reverse side of the picture. Captain Sturt had received a severe wound in the abdomen, from which it was from the first certain he could not recover. He was in great agony; it was impossible to move him without increasing his sufferings, equally impossible that he should not be moved. He was placed in a kind of rough litter, the jolting of which was a terrible aggravation of his pain. At night he lay on a bank in the snow, suffering from intolerable thirst; the water for which he craved could only be supplied, a few spoonfuls at a time, because his wife and mother had no means of getting a larger quantity. Those who have known what it is, even in the midst of every home comfort, to stand by the death-bed of those they love, can best imagine what it was to Lady Sale and her daughter to see the anguish and death of their son and husband under such circumstances as these. The horrors of the retreat became worse and worse. All the baggage was lost, and the whole road was covered with men, women, and children lying down in the

snow to die.

Again Akbar renewed his demand for the women and children, and this time he urged it on grounds of humanity. It now appeared certain that the only chance of saving their lives was to accept Akbar's proposals. Nine ladies, twenty gentlemen, and fourteen children were accordingly made over to him as prisoners or hostages. It is true that he assured them that they were to consider themselves his honoured guests, and that on the whole he behaved well to them, but their sufferings while in his charge were very considerable. They believed themselves to be in constant danger of death, or else that they would be sold as slaves and sent to Bokhara. All their arms and means of defence were taken from them, and they were but too well acquainted with the treacherous and cruel nature of the man whose prisoners they were.

The most noticeable feature of Lady Sale's journal is its buoyant courage and cheerfulness. The forty-three persons of whom the hostages consisted were reinforced by the birth of three infants, one of which was Mrs. Sturt's, and consequently was Lady Sale's grandchild. They were eight and a half months in captivity. Their accommodation very often consisted of no more than two small rooms among the whole party. Lady Sale speaks of being lodged twenty-one in a room fourteen feet by ten feet; another time thirty-four persons had to share a room only fifteen feet by twelve feet; sixteen persons, of both sexes and all ages, shared one small room for a long time. Lady Sale and her daughter—indeed, most of the captives —had lost everything but the clothes they stood in. Yet, in the midst of all the discomfort and danger to which the party was exposed, there is seldom a word of complaint in Lady Sale's journal which she wrote at the time, and more often than not their hardships are turned into matter of laughter and merriment. The retreat from Cabul was begun, it will be remembered, on 6th January; on the 9th the ladies and children, with twenty gentlemen, among whom was Major Lawrence, were made over to Akbar Khan; not until 18th January were they established in permanent quarters in the fort of Buddeeabad. The journal for 19th January begins: "We luxuriated in dressing, although we had no clothes but those on our backs; but we enjoyed washing our faces very much, having had but one opportunity of doing so since we left Cabul. It was rather a painful process, as the cold and glare of the sun on the snow had three times peeled my face, from which the skin came off in strips." Major Lawrence describes the rooms assigned to the ladies as miserable sheds full of fleas and bugs." But even these and worse trials to the temper were good-humouredly encountered. "It was above ten days," Lady Sale wrote, "after our departure from Cabul before I had an opportunity to change my clothes, or even to take them off and put them on again and wash myself; and fortunate were those who did not possess much live stock. It was not till our arrival here (near Cabul, almost at the end of their captivity) that we completely got rid of *lice,* which we denominated infantry; the fleas, for which Afghanistan is famed, we called light cavalry." The food served out to the prisoners was the reverse of appetising: greasy skin and bones, boiled in the same pot with rice, and all served together, was a usual dish. Lady Sale describes a kind of bread made of unpollarded flour mixed with water, and dried by being set up on edge near a fire. "Eating these cakes of dough," she says, "is a capital recipe for heartburn." The bad cooking they remedied by obtaining leave to cook for themselves.

One of the chief alleviations of their lot consisted—so far, at least, as the ladies were concerned—in needlework; they were supplied with calico, chintz, and other materials, and were most thankful, not only for the clothes which they were thus enabled to make, but also for the occupation the work afforded. The ladies also cheerfully bore their part in other kinds of work, and became laundresses, cooks, and housemaids, and, in one instance, carpenters and masons for the nonce. The choice of rooms

being very limited, one was allotted to Lady Sale and her companions which had no windows, and consequently no means of getting air and light, except what came through the door. "We soon *set to,"* writes Lady Sale, "and by dint of hard working with sticks and stones, in which I bore my part, assisted by Mr. Melville, until both of us got blistered hands, we knocked two small windows out of the wall, and thus obtained 'darkness visible.'" Lady Sale had permission to correspond with her husband, General Sir Robert Sale, who was conducting vigorous measures against the enemy at Jellalabad. Lady Sale was very proud of her husband, and mentions with evident delight the nickname of " Fighting Bob," which his soldiers had given him. Any recognition of his deserts gave her keen satisfaction. She refers to the presentation of a sword to him as "the only thing that has given me pleasure," although at that time her praises were upon everybody's lips. She was so thoroughly a soldier's wife that she understood military tactics: before she left Cabul she speaks of taking up a post of observation on the roof of the house, "as usual," in order to watch the military movements that were going forward. She says she understood the plan of attack as well as she understood the hemming of a handkerchief; therefore she diligently wrote an account of everything of importance to her husband. These letters were so important for the military and political news they contained that they were often forwarded to the Commander-in-chief, to Lord Auckland, the Governor-general, and to the Court of Directors of the East India Company.

The principal danger to which the prisoners were exposed, next to the ferocity and treachery of Akbar Khan's character, arose from the extraordinary frequency of earthquakes in the region in which they were confined. Lady Sale is one of the very few human beings who has ever made such an entry in a journal as this: "3d and 4th March. Earthquakes as usual." Under other dates such expressions as "Earthquakes in plenty" are frequent; and hardly less

significant is the entry, under the date of 19th April, "No earthquakes to-day." The earthquakes were of a most formidable character. Lady Sale had a narrow escape of destruction from one which took place in February. She was on the roof of the room she lived in, hanging out some clothes to dry, when the whole building began to rock; she felt the roof was giving way, and rushed down the stairs, just in time to save her life, as the building fell with an awful crash the instant she left it. Lawrence writes: "We all assembled in the centre of the court, as far from the crumbling walls as possible,... when suddenly the entire structure disappeared as through a trap-door, disclosing to us a yawning chasm. The stoutest hearts among us quailed at the appalling sight, for the world seemed coming to an end."

Almost the only angry words that appear in Lady Sale's journal are caused by attempts of the officers to negotiate a ransom for themselves and the rest of the party, without consulting the ladies as to the terms to be agreed upon. Women's suffrage had not been much talked of in 1842, but Lady Sale appeared to hold that taxation and representation ought to go hand in hand; for she says, "A council of officers was held at the General's regarding this same ransom business, which they refer to Macgregor. I protest against being implicated in any proceedings in which I have no vote." In the end the Indian Government paid the sum that it was agreed to give to Saleh Mahomed for effecting the deliverance of the prisoners. Another source of irritation to Lady Sale was the dread lest the military authorities should hesitate to proceed vigorously against the Afghans at the right moment because it might endanger the lives of the hostages. "Now is the time," she wrote on the 10th May, "to strike the blow, but I much dread dilly-dallying just because a handful of us are in Akbar's power. What are *our* lives compared with the honour of our country *!* Not that I am at all inclined to have my throat cut; on the contrary, I hope I shall live to see the British flag once more triumphant in Afghanistan."

Allusion has already been made to Lady Sale's power of extracting grim fun out of the discomforts of the situation. The Afghans are great thieves, and one of the minor troubles of the captives lay in the fact that their captors calmly appropriated articles sent to the prisoners. They took possession of a case in which Lady Sale had left some small bottles. "I hope," she writes, "the Afghans will try their contents as medicine, and find them efficacious: one bottle contained nitric acid, another a strong solution of lunar caustic." Twice she was incapacitated by severe attacks of fever, which had proved fatal to several of the party; but her courage never deserted her; and she shook off fever and all other ills when she heard her husband was near. Saleh Mahomed had already agreed, for a sum of money, to remove them from Akbar's power, and they had left the place in which they had been confined; but Akbar would probably have recaptured them had not Sir R. Sale and Sir R. Shakespear with their brigades joined them just at the nick of time.

Who can tell what the meeting must have been between the gallant husband and wife? The narrative can best be given in Lady Sale's own words: "Had we not received assistance, our recapture was certain.... It is impossible to express our feelings on Sale's approach. To my daughter and myself happiness, so long delayed as to be almost unexpected, was actually painful, and accompanied by a choking sensation which could not obtain the relief of tears. When we arrived where the infantry were posted, they cheered all the captives as they passed them, and the men of the 13th" (her husband's regiment) "pressed forward to welcome us individually. Most of the men had a little word of hearty congratulation to offer each in his own style on the restoration of his colonel's wife and daughter; and then my highly-wrought feelings found the desired relief; I could scarcely speak to thank the soldiers for their sympathy, whilst the long-withheld tears now found their course."

ELIZABETH GILBEET

Elizabeth Gilbert, daughter of the

Bishop of Chichester, was one of the blind who help the blind. It is true, physically, that the blind cannot lead the blind; but, perhaps, none are so well fitted as the blind, who are gifted with courage, sympathy, and hope, to show the way to careers of happy and active usefulness to those who are suffering from a similar calamity with themselves.

The Bishop's little daughter, born at Oxford in 1826, was not blind from her birth. She is described in the first years of infancy as possessing dark flashing eyes, that, no doubt, were as eager to see and know as other baby eyes. Her sight was taken from her by an attack of scarlet fever when she was two years and eight months old. Her mother had lately been confined, and, consequently, was entirely isolated from the little invalid. The care of the child devolved upon her father, who nursed her most tenderly, and, by his ceaseless watchfulness and care, probably saved her life. But when the danger to life was passed, it was found that the poor little girl had lost her sight. Everything was done that could be done; the most skilful oculists and physicians of the day were consulted, but could do nothing except confirm the fears of her parents that their little girl was blind for life.

With this one great exception of blindness, Elizabeth Gilbert's childhood was peculiarly happy and fortunate. Her parents wisely determined to educate her, as much as possible, with their other children, and to avoid everything which could bring into prominence that she was not as the others were. There was a large family of the Gilbert children, and Bessie, as she was always called, like the others, was required to dress herself and wait on herself in many little ways that bring out a child's independence and helpfulness. She used to sit always by her father's side at dessert, and pour him out a glass of wine, which she did very cleverly without spilling a drop. When asked how she could do this, she replied it was quite easy —she judged by the weight when the glass was full. She learnt French, German, Italian, and music,

with her sisters, and joined them in their games, both indoors and out. When she required special watching and care, they were given silently, without letting her find out that she was being singled out for protection. When she was old enough, the direction of the household and other domestic duties were entrusted to her in her parents' absence, in turn with her other sisters. Thus her ardour, relf-reliance, and courage were undamped, and she was prepared for the life's work to which she afterwards devoted herself— the industrial training of the adult blind. In 1842 an event happened which doubtless had a good effect in developing Miss Gilbert's natural independence of character, which had been so carefully preserved by her parents training. Her godmother died and left her a considerable sum of money, of which she was to enjoy the income as soon as she came of age. It was, therefore, in her power to carry out the scheme which she formed in after years for the benefit of the blind, without being obliged to rely at the outset on others for pecuniary support. She never could have done what she did if she had been obliged to ask her parents for the money the development of her plans necessarily required. They were most kindly and wisely generous to her, but it would have been impossible to one of her honourable and sensitive nature to spend

K freely and liberally as she did money which was not her own. The saddest and most desponding period of her life was that which came after she had ceased to be a child, and before she had taken up the life's work to which reference has just been made. She was one of a bevy of eight sisters; and they naturally, as they passed from childhood to womanhood, entered more and more into a world which was closed to their blind sister. At that time, even more than now, marriage was the one career for which all young women were consciously or unconsciously preparing. It was hard for a young girl to live in a social circle in which marriage was looked upon as the one honourable goal of female ambition, and to feel at the same time that it was one from which she was herself debarred. Those who saw her at this time, say she would often sit silent and apart in the drawing-room of her father's house in Queen Anne Street, with the tears streaming down her face, and that she would spend hours together on her knees weeping. "To the righteous there ariseth a light in darkness." The light-bringers to the sad heart of Bessie Gilbert were manifold; and as is usual in such cases, the light of her own life was found in working for the welfare of others. The most healing and cheering of words to those who are sick at heart are, "Come and work in My vineyard."

Small things often help great ones; and a clever mechanical invention by a Frenchman named Foucault, for enabling blind people to write, was not an unimportant link in the chain that drew Miss Gilbert out of her despondency. By means of this writing frame, she entered into correspondence with a young blind man, named William Hanks Levy, who had lately married the matron of the St. John's Wood School for the Blind. Levy entered with great zeal, enthusiasm, and originality into all the schemes Miss Gilbert began to form for the welfare of the blind. Her thoughts were further turned in the direction of working for the blind poor, by a book called *Meliora,* written by Lord Ingestre, the aim of which was to show how the gulf between rich and poor could be bridged over. But most important of all, perhaps, of the influences that were making a new outlook for her life, was her friendship with Miss Bathurst, daughter of Sir James Bathurst. This lady was deeply interested in all efforts to raise up and improve the lot of women, and especially devoted herself to opening the means of higher education to them. She was one of those who hoped all things and believed all things, and, consequently, she rebelled against the impious notion that if a woman were not married there was no use or place for her in the world. It was her clear strong faith in women's work and in women's worth, that helped more than anything else to give dignity, purpose, and happiness to Bessie Gil-

bert's life. The life of the blind girl became ennobled by the purpose to work for the good of others, and to help both women and men who were afflicted similarly with herself to make the best use of their lives that circumstances permitted.

Very little, comparatively, at that time had been done for the blind. The excellent college at Norwood did not exist. The poor blind very frequently became beggars, and the well-to-do blind, with few exceptions, were regarded as doomed to a life of uselessness; in some instances, as in Miss Gilbert's own, kindly and intelligent men thought it neither wrong nor unnatural to express a hope that " the Almighty would take the child who was afflicted with blindness." What was specially needed at the time Miss Gilbert's attention was directed to the subject was the means of industrial training, to enable those who had lost their sight in manhood or womanhood to earn their own living. The proficiency of the blind in music is well known, but to attain a high degree of excellence in this requires a training from early childhood. To those who become blind in infancy a musical education affords the best chance of future independence; but thousands become blind in later life, when they are too old to acquire professional skill as musicians; and, besides these, there are those who are too completely without the taste for music to render it possible for them to become either performers or teachers of it. It was especially for the poor adult blind that Miss Gilbert laboured. She studied earnestly to discover the various kinds of manual labour in which the blind stood at the least disadvantage in comparison with sighted persons. Her efforts had a humble beginning, for the first shop she opened was in a cellar in Holborn, which she rented at Is. 6d. a week. She was ably seconded by Levy, and by a blind carpenter named Farrar; the cellar was used as a store for the mats, baskets, and brushes made by blind people in their own homes. A move was, however, soon made to a small house near Brunswick Square, but the work soon

outgrew these premises also, and a house was taken, with a shop and workrooms, in what is now the Euston Road. Miss Gilbert exerted herself assiduously to promote the sale of the articles made by her clients. The goods were sold at the usual retail price, and their quality was in many respects superior to that of similar goods offered in ordinary shops; in this way a regular circle of customers was in time obtained, who were willing to buy of the blind what the blind were able to produce. It must not be supposed, however, that this process, which sounds so easy and simple in words, was really easy and simple in practice. The blind men and women had to be taught their trades; in the case of many of them, their health was below the average, and, in the case of a few, they were not quite clear that working had any advantages over begging, for a living. Miss Gilbert and her foreman, W. Levy, had industrial, physical, and moral difficulties to contend with that would have daunted any who were less firmly grounded in the belief in the permanent usefulness of what they had undertaken. Miss Gilbert found that many of the blind people she employed could not, with the best will in the world, earn enough to support themselves. The deficiency was for years made up from her own private means. W. Levy had what. appears a mistaken enthusiasm for employing none but blind persons in the various industries carried on in the workshop. There are some industrial processes for performing which blindness is an absolute bar, some in which it is a great disadvantage, others in which it is a slight disadvantage, and a few in which it is no disadvantage at all. The aim of those who wish to benefit the blind should be, in my judgment, to promote co-operation of labour between the blind and the seeing, so that to the blind may be left those processes in which the loss of sight places them at the least disadvantage. The blind Milton composed *Paradise Lost,* and other noble poems, which will live as long as the English language lasts. He never could have done this if the mechanical labour of writing down his compositions had not been given over to those who had the use of their eyes. This is an extreme instance, but it may be taken as an example of the way in which the blind and the seeing should work together, each doing the best their natural faculties and limitations fit them for. Levy had an intense pride in having everything in Miss Gilbert's institution done only by the blind. So far did he carry this prejudice that it was only with difficulty that he was induced to have a seeing assistant for keeping the accounts. Previous to this, as was natural and inevitable, they were in the most hopeless confusion. Levy was, however, in many ways an invaluable leader and fellowworker. His courage and energy were boundless. On one occasion he undertook successfully a journey to France in order to discover the place where some pretty baskets were made. He and his wife landed at Calais almost entirely ignorant of the French language, and knowing nothing except that certain baskets, for which there was then a good demand in England, were being manufactured in one of the eighty-nine departments of France. After many wanderings, both accidental and inevitable, he discovered the place. He was received with great kindness by the people who made the baskets, and, having learnt how to make them himself, he returned to England to communicate his knowledge to his and Miss Gilbert's company of blind workpeople. A letter of Levy's to Miss Gilbert, describinga fire that had broken out close to the institution, and had for some time placed it in great danger, is a wonderful instance of a blind man's energy and power of acting promptly and courageously in the face of danger.

Little by little the work Miss Gilbert had begun grew and prospered. A regular society was formed, of which the Queen became the patron, and of which Miss Gilbert was the most active and devoted member. This association received the name of the Society for Promoting the General Welfare of the Blind. Its present habitation is in Berners Street, London. Its founder, for several years before her death, was obliged, through ill-health, to withdraw from all active participation in its business; but so well and firmly had she laid the foundations, that others were able to carry on what she had begun. The Society is one of the most useful in London for the poor adult blind, because it provides them with industrial training, according to their individual capacities, and secures them, as far as possible, a constant and regular market for the goods they are able to produce. The wages earned are in some cases supplemented by small grants, and pensions are, in several instances, given to those blind men and women who have survived their power of work. The result of Miss Gilbert's life has been to ameliorate very much the lot of the blind poor by substituting the means of self-supporting industry for the doles and alms which at one time were looked upon as the only means of showing kindness and pity to the blind. Miss Gilbert herself was keenly sensible of the value and life-giving power of work. Surrounded as she had been from childhood with every care and kindness which loving and generous parents could suggest, she yet found that when she began to work, the change was like a passing from death to life. The book from which all the facts and details in this sketch are taken tells that soon after she began her work one of her *Elizabeth Gilbert and Her Work for the Blind.* By Frances Martin. Macmillan and Co.

friends "hoped she was not working herself to death." She replied, with a happy laugh, "Work myself to death ⁄ I am working myself to life." It is just this possibility of "working to life" that she has placed within the reach of so many blind men and women.

Miss Gilbert's health was always very fragile. After 1872 she became by degrees a confirmed invalid, and after much suffering, borne with exquisite patience and cheerfulness, she died early in the year 1885.

JANE AUSTEN

There is very little story to tell in the life of Jane Austen. She was one of the greatest writers of English fiction; but her own life, like the life she describes with such extraordinary and minute accuracy in her tales, had no startling incidents, no catastrophes. The solid ground never shook beneath her feet; neither she, nor the relations and neighbours with whom her tranquil life was passed, were ever swept away by the whirlwind of wild 'passions, nor overwhelmed by tragic destiny. The ordinary, everyday joys and sorrows that form a part of the lives of all of us, were hers; but nothing befell her more sensational or wondrous than what falls to the lot of most of us. This even tenor of her own way she reproduces with marvellous skill in the pages of her novels. It has been well said that "every village could furnish matter for a novel to Miss Austen." The material which she used is within the reach of every one; but she stands alone, hitherto quite unequalled, for the power of investing with charm and interest these incidents in the everyday life of everyday people which are the whole subject-matter of her six finished novels. A silly elopement on the part of one of the five Miss Bennets in *Pride and Prejudice,* and the fall which stuns Louisa Musgrove in *Persuasion,* when she insists on jumping off the cob at Lyme, are almost the only incidents in her books that can even be called unusual. Her novels remind us of pictures we sometimes see which contain no one object of supreme or extraordinary loveliness, but which charm by showing us the beauty and interest in that which lies around us on every side. There is a picture by Frederick Walker, called "A Rainy Day," which is a very good instance of this; it is nothing but a village street just by a curve in the road; the houses are such as may be seen in half the villages in England: a dog goes along looking as dejected as dogs always do in the rain, the light is reflected in the puddles of the wet road, one foot-passenger only has ventured out. There is nothing in the picture but what we may all of us have seen hundreds and thousands of times, and yet one could look and look at it for hours and never weary of the charm of quiet, truthful beauty it contains. This is one of the things which true artists, whether their art is painting pictures or writing books, can do for those who are not artists—that is, help them to see and feel the beauty and interest of the ordinary surroundings of everyday life. Robert Browning makes a great Italian painter say— We're made so that we love

First when we see them painted, things we have passed

Perhaps a hundred times nor oared to see;

And so they are better painted—better to us,

Which is the same thing. Art was given for that;

God uses us to help each other so,

Lending our minds out. Have you noticed, now,

Your cullion's hanging face? A bit of chalk,

And trust me, but you should, though! How much more

If I drew higher things with the same truth!

That were to take the Prior's pulpit place,

Interpret God to all of you.

Jane Austen was a clergyman's daughter, born in 1775 at the Vicarage of Steventon, about seven miles from A very interesting memoir of Miss Austen lias been written by her nephew, Mr. Austen Leigh. All who love her works should read it, and thereby come to know and love the woman.

Basingstoke, in Hampshire. Here she lived, for the first twenty-five years of her life, the quiet family life of most young ladies of similar circumstances; two of her brothers were in the Navy, one was a country gentleman, having inherited an estate from a cousin, another was a clergyman. The most dearly loved by Jane of all her family was her sister Cassandra, older than herself by three years. The sisters were so inseparable that when Cassandra went to school, Jane, though too young to profit much by the instruction given, was sent also, because it would have been cruel to separate the sisters; her mother said, "If Cassandra were going to have her head cut off, Jane would insist on sharing her fate." The devotion between the sisters was lifelong. Their characters were not much alike; Cassandra was

colder, calmer, and more reserved than her sister, whose sweet temper and affectionate disposition specially endeared her to all her family; but Jane throughout her life relied upon Cassandra as one who was wiser and stronger than herself. The quiet family life at Steventon was diversified by one or two visits to Bath, then a very fashionable resort; a short visit to Lyme is spoken of later on; and in the early days in the vicarage the Austen children not infrequently amused themselves with private theatricals. Readers of *Northanger Abbey, Persuasion,* and *Mansfield Park* will find these mild amusements woven into the web of the story; for, as Jane Austen says herself, she was like a bird who uses the odd bits of wool or moss in the hedgerows near to weave into the tiny fabric of its nest. The plays which the Austens acted were frequently written by themselves. This may probably have given to Jane her early impulse to authorship. It is not improbable that it also smoothed the way of her career as a writer in another sense; for at that time very great prejudice still existed in many people's minds against women who were writers. Lord Granville, speaking in December 1887, at the unveiling of the statue of the Queen at Holloway College, cited a great French writer who had laid it down as an axiom that a woman could commit no greater fault than to be learned; the same writer had said—of course partly in joke—that it is enough knowledge for any woman if she is acquainted with the fact that Pekin is not in Europe, or that Alexander the Great was not the son-in-law of Louis the XIV. Referring to events within his own knowledge and memory, Lord Granville added, "One of the most eminent English statesmen of the century, a brilliant man of letters himself, after reading with admiration a beautiful piece of poetry written by his daughter, appealed to her affection for him to prevent her ever writing again, his fear was so great lest she should be thought a literary woman."

If a similar prejudice were in any degree felt by the Austen family, it is not unlikely that it was gradually dissolved

by the early habit of the children of writing plays for home acting. We read, indeed, that Jane did nearly all her writing in the general sitting-room of the family, and that she was careful to keep her occupation secret from all but her own immediate relations. For this purpose she wrote on small pieces of paper, which could easily be put away, or covered by a piece of blotting-paper or needlework. The little mahogany desk at which she wrote is still preserved in the family. She never put her name on a title-page, but there is no evidence that her family would have disapproved of her doing so. They seem to have delighted in all she did, and to have helped her by every means in their power. She was a great favourite with her brothers and sister, and with all the tribe of nephews and nieces that grew up about her. She had no trace of any assumption of superiority, and gave herself no airs of any kind. She had too much humour and sense of fun for there to be any danger of this in her case. She was thoroughly womanly in her habits, manners, and occupations. Like Miss Martineau, her early training preserved her from being a literary lady who could not sew. Her needlework was remarkably fine and dainty, and specimens of it are still preserved which show that her fingers had the same deftness and skill as the mind which created Emma Woodhouse and her father, Mrs. Norris and Elizabeth Bennet. She had taken to authorship as a duck takes to water, and had written some of her most remarkable books before she was twenty; and she had done this so simply and naturally that she seems to have produced in her family the impression that writing first-rate novels was one of the easiest things in the world. We find, for instance, that she writes in 1814 many letters of advice to a novel-writing niece; and she advises another little niece to cease writing till she is sixteen years old, the child being at that time only ten or twelve. In 1816 she addresses a very interesting letter to a nephew who is writing a novel, and has had the misfortune to lose two chapters and a half! She makes kindly fun of the young gentleman, and suggests that if she finds his lost treasure she shall engraft his chapters into her own novel, but she adds: "I do not think, however, that any theft of that sort would be really very useful to me. What should I do with your strong, manly, vigorous sketches, full of variety and glow? How' could I possibly join them on to the little bit (two inches wide) of ivory on which I work with so fine a brush as produces little effect after much labour?"

Early in 1801 the home at Steventon was broken up. Mr. Austen resigned his living in consequence of failing health, and the family removed to Bath. Mr. Austen died in 1805, and Mrs. Austen and her daughters lived for a time at Southampton. They had no really home-like home, however, between leaving Steventon in 1801 and settling at Chawton, in Hampshire, in 1809; and it is very characteristic of Jane Austen's home-loving nature that this homeless period was also a period of literary inactivity. She wrote *Sense and Sensibility, Northanger Abbey,* and *Pride and Prejudice* before she left Steventon, though none of them were published till after she came to live at Chawton. Here in her second home she wrote *Mansfield Park, Emma,* and *Persuasion.* In consequence of having three novels finished before one was printed, when she once began to publish, her works appeared in rapid succession. *Sense and Sensibility* was the first to appear, in 1811, and the others followed quickly after one another, for her work was at once appreciated by the public, and the great leaders of the literary world, such as Sir Walter Scott, Southey, and Coleridge, welcomed her with cordial and generous praise. One curious little adventure should be mentioned. In 1803, during her residence at Bath, she had sold the manuscript of *Northanger Abbey* to a Bath publisher for £10. This good man, on reconsideration, evidently thought he had made a bad bargain, and resolved to lose his ten pounds rather than risk a larger sum in printing and publishing the book. The manuscript therefore lay on his shelves for many years quite forgotten. But the time came when *Sense and Sensibility,*

Pride and Prejudice, and *Mansfield Park* had placed their author in the first rank of English writers, and it occurred to Miss Austen and her family that it might be well to rescue *Northanger Abbey* from its unappreciative possessor. One of her brothers called on the Bath publisher and negotiated with him the re-purchase of the manuscript, giving for it the same sum which had been paid to the author about ten years earlier. The publisher was delighted to get back his £10, which he had never expected to see again, and Jane Austen's brother was delighted to get back the manuscript. Both parties to the bargain were fully satisfied; but the poor publisher's feelings would have been very different if he had known that the neglected manuscript, with which he had so joyfully parted, was by the author of the most successful novels of the day.

There is a quiet vein of fun and humorous observation running through all Miss Austen's writings. It is as visible in her private letters to her friends as in her works intended for publication. The little turns of expression are not reproduced, but the humour of the one is very similar to that of the other. Thus, for instance, in one of her letters she describes a visit to a young lady at school in London. Jane Austen had left her a raw schoolgirl, and found her, on this visit, developed into a fashionable young lady. "Her hair," writes Jane to Cassandra, "is done up with an elegance to do credit to any education." Who can read this without thinking of Fanny Price in *Mansfield Park,* and the inevitable contempt she inspired in her fashionable cousins because she did not know French and had but one sash?

Reference has already been made to the high appreciation of Miss Austen's genius which has been expressed by the highest literary authorities in her own time and in ours. Sir Walter Scott wrote in his journal: "I have read again, and for the third time, Miss Austen's very finely-written novel of *Pride and Prejudice.* That young lady has a talent for describing the involvements and feelings and characters of ordinary life, which is to me the most wonderful I ever met

with. The big Bow-Wow strain I can do myself like any now going, but the exquisite touch which renders commonplace things and characters interesting from the truth of the descriptive and the sentiment is denied to me." Lord Macaulay, the great historian, wrote in his diary: "Read Dickens's *Hard Times,* and another book of Pliny's *Letters.* Read *Northanger Abbey,* worth all Dickens and Pliny put together. Yet it was the work of a girl. She was certainly not more than twenty-six. Wonderful creature!" Guizot, the French historian, was a great novel reader, and he delighted in English novels, especially those written by women. Referring to the women writers of the beginning of this century, of whom Miss Austen was the chief, he said that their works "form a school which, in the excellence and profusion of its productions, resembles the cloud of dramatic authors of the great Athenian age." The late Mr. Gr. H. Lewes said he would rather have written *Pride and Prejudice* than any of the Waverley novels. George Eliot calls Jane Austen the greatest artist that has ever written, "using the term 'artist' to signify the most perfect master over the means to her end." It is perhaps only fair to state that some good judges do not entertain so high an opinion of her work. Madame de Stael pronounced against her, using the singularly inappropriate word "vulgar," in condemnation of her work. If there is a writer in the world free from vulgarity in its ordinary sense, it is Jane Austen it must be supposed that Madame de Stael used the word in its French sense, *i.e.* "commonplace" or "ordinary," such a meaning of the word as is retained in our English expression "the vulgar tongue." Charlotte Bronte felt in Miss Austen a deficiency in poetic imagination, in the high tone of sentiment which elevates the prose of everyday life into poetry. She found her "shrewd and observant rather than sagacious and profound." Miss Austen's writings were so essentially different from the highly imaginative work of her sister author, that it is not surprising that the younger failed somewhat in appreciation of the elder writer.

Jane Austen's failing health in 1816 caused much anxiety to her family. It is characteristic of her gentle thoughtfulness for all about her that she never could be induced to use the one sofa with which the family sittingroom was provided. Her mother, who was more than seventy years old, often used the sofa, and Jane would never occupy it, even in her mother's absence, preferring to contrive for herself a sort of couch formed with two or three chairs. A little niece, puzzled that "Aunt Jane" preferred this arrangement, drew from her the explanation that if she used the sofa in her mother's absence, Mrs. Austen would probably abstain from using it as much as was good for her. Her last book, *Persuasion,* was finished while she was suffering very much from what proved to be her dying illness. Weak health did not in any way diminish her industry, and she exacted from herself the utmost perfection that she felt she was capable of giving to her work. The last chapters of *Persuasion* were cancelled and re-written because her first conclusion of the story did not satisfy her. In May 1817 she and her sister removed to Winchester in order that Jane might have skilled medical advice. Here she died on 18th July and was buried opposite Wykeham's Chantry, in the cathedral. Her sweetness of temper and her gentle gaiety never failed her throughout a long and trying illness. When the end was near, one of those with her asked if there was anything she wanted; her reply was, "*Nothing hit death.*" MARIA EDGEWOBTH

It will be impossible, in the short limits of these pages, to give anything like a full account of the long life of Maria Edgeworth. She lived for nearly eighty-three years, from 1st January 1767 to 22d May 1849; and through her own and her father's friends she was brought into touch with nearly all the leading men and women connected with the stirring political and literary events of that period. What this implies will be best realised if we consider that her lifetime comprised the whole period of the French Revolution, the War of Independence in the United States, the long

wars of England with Napoleon, the landing of the French in Ireland (her native country), the passing of the Act of Union between England and Ireland, Catholic Emancipation, the Abolition of Slavery in the British Dominions, the passing of the first Reform Bill, the Irish Famine of 1847, and the outbreak of revolutionary socialism on the Continent in 1848. These are some of the most burning of the political events of which she was a witness; the literary and social history of the same period is hardly less remarkable. She lived in the centre of a world made brilliant by Wordsworth, Coleridge, Shelley, Byron, Burns, Keats, Scott, and Jane Austen. She knew Mrs. Fry, Wilberforce, and Sydney Smith, as representing some of the most important of the social movements of her time;

L among her friends in the scientific world were Ricardo, the political economist, Darwin, the naturalist, whose fame has been overshadowed by that of his grandson, the great Charles Darwin of our own times, Sir Humphry Davy, the Herschels, Mrs. Somerville, and James Mill. She knew Mrs. Siddons, and heard her recite in her own house the part of Queen Katherine in the play of *Henry the Eighth.* She was the intimate friend, and connection by marriage, of "Kitty Pakenham," the first Duchess of Wellington, wife of "the Great Duke." She lived to see the old stage coaches supplanted by our modern railways; she was the interested eyewitness of the gradual introduction of the steam-engine into all departments of industry, a change which Sir Walter Scott said he looked on "half proud, half sad, half angry, and half pleased." She might well feel, as old age approached, that she had "warmed both hands at the fire of life." No life could have been fuller than hers of every sort of interest and activity. She said in a letter to a friend, written after a dangerous illness: "When I felt it was more than probable that I should not recover, with a pulse above 120, and at the entrance of my seventysixth year, I was not alarmed. I felt ready to rise tranquil from the banquet of life, where I had been a happy

guest. I confidently relied on the goodness of my Creator " *(Study of Maria Edgeworth,* by Grace A. Oliver, p. 521).

Maria Edgeworth's family was one of English origin, which had settled in Ireland in the reign of Queen Elizabeth. The Edgeworths intermarried into Irish, Welsh, and English families, but always maintained strong Irish sympathies.

There were many remarkable men and women in the Edgeworth family before the birth of our heroine, but space forbids the mention of more than one, her father, Richard Lovell Edgeworth, whose name and fame are intimately associated with those of his daughter. Mr. Edgeworth was a most extraordinary man; at one moment one admires him, at another one laughs at him, but one must always be astonished by him "To put a girdle round about the earth in forty minutes" would have been a congenial task to him. He made clocks, built bridges, raised spires, invented telegraphs, manufactured balloons, ink, and soap, constructed locks on his bedroom doors of such a complicated nature, that his guests were afraid to shut their doors lest they never should be able to open them again.

When on a journey in France about 1770, he stayed at Lyons, and carried out a plan for diverting the Rhone from its course, thereby saving a large tract of country that had previously been inaccessible; for this service the city of Lyons rewarded him by a grant of land; this property, however, was confiscated a few years later during the Revolution.

He raised a corps of volunteer infantry in Ireland, to which Roman Catholics as well as Protestants were admitted, although at that time the sentiment of religious equality was regarded as akin to infidelity and disloyalty. He was born in England, and educated partly here and partly in Ireland; like most of the Edgeworths, he came of a mixed race, his mother being a Welsh woman of considerable literary acquirements and faculties; his first remarkable performance was a runaway marriage, which he contracted at the age of nineteen, with a Miss Elers, a lady of German origin, whom he appears rather to have disliked than otherwise. A runaway marriage with a girl whom he really loved would have been too commonplace a proceeding in those days for this eccentric young gentleman. Speaking of this lady, Mr. Edgeworth wrote: "My wife was prudent, domestic, and affectionate, but she was not of a cheerful temper. She lamented about trifles; and the lamenting of a female, with whom we live, does not render home delightful." It is not recorded if Mrs. Edgeworth found the lamenting of the male with whom she lived any more delightful, nor indeed is it evident that her husband devoted much of his overflowing energy to lamentation. As he did not find his home delightful, he spent very little time in it, and was not long before he found pleasant society elsewhere.

One can never think of Mr. Edgeworth apart from his extraordinary domestic history. He had four wives, one after another, in rapid succession, and twenty-two children. There were four children, of whom Maria was one, by the first marriage with the "lamenting female." The eldest of these, born when his father was under twenty, was brought up on the principles advocated by Rousseau, which may perhaps be summarised as never forcing a child to do anything that he does not wish to do. One experiment of this kind appears to have sufficed for the family; the other twenty-one children, or such of them as survived infancy, were treated according to other theories. Indeed, it seems to have been part of Maria's education that she was to undertake, for a part of every day, some study or occupation that was uncongenial to her. Mr. Edgeworth's theories of education seem to have been almost as numerous as his family; a story is told in the book already quoted, of the visit of a gentleman to Edgeworthstown House in Ireland; on rejoining the ladies after dinner, the guest was imprudent enough to exclaim on the beauty of the golden hair of one of the younger girls. Mr. Edgeworth instantly took his daughter by the hand, walked across the room, opened a drawer, held her head over it, and with a large pair of scissors cut off all her hair

close to her head. "As the golden ringlets fell into the drawer, this extraordinary father said, 'Charlotte, what do you say V She answered, 'Thank you, father.' Turning to his guests, he remarked, 1 will not allow a daughter of mine to be vain.'"

Among the friendships that had a powerful influence on Mr. Edgeworth's character must be mentioned that with Mr. Day, the author of a book which is still well known, *Sandford and Merton.* Mr. Day was an even more extraordinary man than Mr. Edgeworth. He entirely set at naught all the usual habits of society; we are told that he "seldom combed his raven locks." He professed to think love had been the greatest curse to mankind, and announced in season and out of season his determination never to marry. It appears that the assistance of a great many ladies was needed to help him for a time to keep his word. He made offers of marriage to Margaret Edgeworth, his friend's sister, to Honora and Elizabeth Sneyd (who became later the second and third wives of Mr. Edgeworth); and failing to induce any of these ladies to accept him, he adopted two orphan girls from the Foundling with the object of educating one of them to such a pitch of perfection that she should be fit to be his wife. In order to foster the quality of "fortitude in females," he used to drop hot sealing-wax on their bare arms, and fire off pistols, charged with powder only, at their petticoats. One of the two little girls could never entirely overcome the tendency to make use of some vehement expression of pain or alarm under these circumstances. This Mr. Day considered a fatal disqualification for ever promoting her to be his wife. The other, to whom the romantic name of Sabrina Sydney had been given, was more promising, and at one time it seemed as if the perilous honour of being Mrs. Day would be hers. However, she was saved by her disobedience to his injunctions against wearing a particular kind of sleeve and handkerchief which were then in fashion. Upon this piece of self-will, we are told that " he at once and decidedly gave her up."

Mr. Day's proposals to Honora and Elizabeth Sneyd, two beautiful sisters with whom he and Mr. Edgeworth were brought much in contact at Lichfield, have been already mentioned. Mr. Day pretended to despise beauty and to condemn love; but Honora's beauty so far overcame his prejudices that he at least professed love for her. His offer of marriage, however, was more like an ultimatum of war than an expression of affection. He sent her a huge packet, in which he detailed all the conditions he should expect her to fulfil if she married him. One of these was entire seclusion from all society but his own. She replied that she "would not admit the unqualified control of a husband over all her actions: she did not feel that seclusion from society was indispensably necessary to preserve female virtue, or to secure domestic happiness. And she declined leaving her mode of life for any ' dark and untried system.'" Mr. Day was deeply wounded, but it was his vanity that suffered rather than his heart; for in three weeks he made a similar overture to Honora's sister, Elizabeth. Now, however, the tables were turned. Whether the sisters conspired together to punish him is not known; but Elizabeth imposed conditions on her lover before she would consent to receive his attentions; she declared she could never marry a man who could neither fence, dance, nor ride, and had none of the accomplishments of a gentleman. These were the very qualities Mr. Day had chiefly exercised his philosophy in deriding and denouncing. "How could he," cried Miss Elizabeth, with cruel logic, "with propriety abuse and ridicule talents in which he appeared deficient *l*" Mr. Day therefore repaired to France with Mr. Edgeworth in order to acquire those polite accomplishments of which it had been the pride of his heart to know nothing. Poor Mr. Day!

How many a month I strove to suit
These stubborn fingers to the lute!
To-day I venture all I know.
She will not hear my music? So I
Break the string; fold music's wing:
Suppose Pauline had bade me sing.

When he came back from France,

cruel Elizabeth laughed in his face, and said she had liked him best as he was before. Notwithstanding all these unsuccessful attempts, Mr. Day found a wife at length. She was a lady of large fortune, which, of course, he "despised" and appropriated. She conformed to all her husband's whims, and honestly believed him to be the best and most distinguished of men. "That's what a man wants in a wife mostly," as Mrs. Poyser says; "one who'd pretend she didn't know which end she stood uppermost till her husband told her." Mr. Day fell a victim at last to one of his numerous theories. He disapproved of the professional method of breaking in colts, and undertook to train one upon an improved plan of his own. The animal plunged violently and threw him; he had concussion of the brain, and died a few minutes after his fall. Poor Mrs. Day was so inconsolable that she took to her bed, and died two years later. She must have been a woman of the type of Milton's Eve: "Herself, though fairest, unsupported flower." When her prop was gone, she drooped and died.

During Mr. Edgeworth's residence at Lyons his first wife, Maria's mother, died, and in a few months he married the beautiful Honora Sneyd. The social circle at Lichfield, in which Honora had lived before her marriage, contained many distinguished persons, among them Dr. Darwin, and Miss Anna Seward, the poetess. Honora herself had been engaged, or partly engaged, to Major André, the unfortunate officer whose execution as a spy by the Americans, during the War of Independence, caused such deep indignation in England. Her marriage to Mr. Edgeworth in 1773, and her death in 1780, took place before the melancholy end of Major Andre's life. The association of Honora's name with that of Major Andre is mentioned here as an illustration of the way in which the Edgeworth family were connected, in some form or another, with many of the most interesting events of the times in which they lived. Another such incident is to be found in the fact that the Abbe Edgeworth, a relative who had become a Roman

Catholic priest, and had lived many years in France, attended Louis XVI upon the scaffold, and received his last words.

Of the charm and goodness of the beautiful Honora there can be no doubt. She won all hearts. Her little stepdaughter, Maria, loved her dearly, and admired her as much as she loved her. She remembered, in after years, standing at her step-mother's dressing-table and looking up at her with a sudden thought, "How beautiful!" The second Mrs. Edgeworth became, under her husband's tuition, a very good mechanic; and together they wrote a little book for children, called *Harry and Lucy.* Very few books for children had at that time been written, so that they were very early in a field which has since found so many labourers. Mrs. Honora discerned Maria's remarkable qualities of mind. When the latter was only twelve years old her step-mother wrote to her expressing the pleasure she felt in being able to treat the young girl "as her equal in every respect but age." Mr. Edgeworth, too, fully appreciated and studiously cultivated Maria's gifts, and encouraged her in every way to treat him with openness and familiarity. This conduct was a very great contrast with the extreme stiffness and formality which then prevailed generally between parents and children. It was near this time, but a little later, that the well-known writer, William Godwin, was reproached by his mother with his too great formality in addressing her; he had been accustomed to speak and write to her as "Madam," and she says in one of her letters to him that "Hon'd Mother" "would be full as agreeable." Therefore the terms of friendly familiarity and equality between Maria and her parents were the more remarkable. The happiness of Mr. Edgeworth's second marriage was unclouded, except by the symptoms of consumption in Honora, which warned them that an inevitable parting was at hand. She died in May 1780, when Maria was thirteen years old. By his dead wife's side, Mr. Edgeworth wrote to Maria impressing upon her all the hopes that he and her step-

mother had formed for her future. Very soon after he wrote again and bade her write a short story on the subject of generosity; "It must be taken," he wrote, "from History or Romance, and must be sent the sennight after you receive this; and I beg that you will take some pains about it." The story, when finished, was submitted to the judgment of Mr. William Sneyd, Honora's brother, who said of it, "An excellent story, and extremely well written; but where is the generosity *1*"—a saying which afterwards became a household word with the Edgeworths.

When Honora was dying she had solemnly begged her husband and her sister Elizabeth to marry each other after her own death. Such marriages at that time were not illegal, and eight months after Honora's death her sister and Mr. Edgeworth were married in St. Andrew's Church, Holborn. Not long after this the first really important event of Maria's life took place, when she went with her father, and the rest of his family to take up her residence in her Irish home. At the impressionable age of fifteen, after having lived long enough in England to judge of the differences between the two countries, she was introduced to an intimate acquaintance with rural life in Ireland. Her father employed no agent for the management of his property, but invited and expected Maria to help him in all his business. In this way she acquired a thorough insight into the charm, the weakness and the strength, the humour and the melancholy of the Irish character.

From 1782, when Mr. Edgeworth and his family returned to live at their Irish home, dates not only Maria Edgeworth's close observation of Irish character and customs, but also the very painstaking literary training which she began to receive from her father. Up to this time Maria had been much at school; owing to the delicate health of her first step-mother, it was considered best that her education should be mainly carried on elsewhere than at home. Now, however, Mr. Edgeworth divided his time between the management of his estates and the education of his children, and to Maria's literary education in particular he devoted himself with singular zeal and assiduity. She was continually practised by him in systematic observing and writing; she was instructed to prepare stories in outline. "None of your drapery," her father would say; "I can imagine all that. Let me see the bare skeleton." At this stage her compositions would be altered, revised, and amended by him, and then returned to her for completion.

There is no doubt whatever of the immense pains which Mr. Edgeworth bestowed upon Maria's literary training; and Maria herself felt that she owed everything to him. It may, however, very well be doubted whether his influence upon her was good from the literary point of view. He gave her method and system, and he cultivated her natural faculties for observation; but there was something very mechanical and pedantic in his mind—an affectation, a want of humour, and a want of spontaneity: she, when left to herself, was content with grouping the facts of life and nature as she saw them around her, without trying to be more instructive than they are. *Castle Rackrent,* which is the best of her Irish stories, was entirely her own, and bears no traces of her father's hand. This is the only one of her tales of which she did not draw out a preliminary sketch or framework for her father's criticism. She says herself of this story, "A curious fact, that where I least aimed at drawing characters I succeeded best. As far as I have heard, the characters in *Castle Rackrent* were, in their day, considered as better classes of Irish characters than any I ever drew; they cost me no trouble, and were made by no *receipt,* or thought of philosophical classification; there was literally not a correction, not an alteration, made in the first writing, no copy, and, as I recollect, no interlineation; it went to the press just as it was written. Other stories I have corrected with the greatest care, and remodelled and re-written." If she had given the world more work of this kind, and less of the kind produced under her father's methods, her name would to-day occupy a higher place than it does in the hierarchy of literature.

Maria Edgeworth may be said to have invented the modern novel, which gives the traits, the speech, the manners, and the thoughts of a peasantry instead of moving only among the upper ten thousand. Sir Walter Scott, with his usual frankness and generosity, stated in his preface to the Waverley Novels that what really started him in his career as a novelist was the desire to do for Scotland and the Scottish peasantry what Miss Edgeworth had done for Ireland and the Irish peasantry. "I felt," he said, "that something might be attempted for my own country of the same kind with that which Miss Edgeworth so fortunately achieved for Ireland—something which might introduce her natives to those of the sister kingdom in a more favourable light than they had been placed hitherto, and to tend to procure sympathy for their virtues and indulgence for their foibles." Another of the leading writers of this century has acknowledged his indebtedness to Miss Edgeworth. The great Russian novelist, Ivan Tourgenieff, told a friend that when he was quite young he was unacquainted with the English language, but he used to hear his elder brother reading out to his friends translations of Miss Edgeworth's Irish stories, and the hope rose in his mind that one day he would be able to do for Russia and her people what Miss Edgeworth had done for Ireland.

Readers of the life of Maria Edgeworth find plenty of evidence of the extremely disturbed state of Ireland during the ten or twelve years which immediately preceded the passing of the Act of Union in 1800. Reports of midnight outrages by armed and disguised bands of assassins were frequent; unpopular people were hooted and pelted by day, and sometimes murdered by night; country houses were provided with shutters so contrived as to make it possible to open a cross-fire upon these murderous bands in case of necessity. The "Thrashers" and the "Whitetooths" were the names then assumed by those marauders who in later times have been known as Whiteboys and Moonlighters. The state of Ireland, politically and socially, became so critical that many people began to feel that almost any change must be for the better. Added to all the other elements of confusion, there was, about 1798, the almost daily expectation of the French invasion. England and France were at war, and it was believed by our enemies that if they could once effect a landing in Ireland the people of that island were so ready for rebellion that the landing of the French would be in itself almost enough to place the whole country at their disposal. In this expectation they were, fortunately, very much deceived. A graphic description of the French invasion, and its utter failure to accomplish its purpose, has been given by Miss Edgeworth. Her family had, indeed, a very close acquaintance with the rebels and the invaders. The county in which Edgeworthstown was situated was in actual insurrection, and when the French landed at Killala, in county Mayo, they marched immediately upon Longford, which was in close proximity to Edgeworthstown.

Mr. Edgeworth sent to the nearest garrison for military protection for his household. He also found the majority of the troop of infantry which he had organised faithful to him; but it soon became evident, in spite of this and of the personal fidelity of his servants and tenants, that the house must be abandoned, and that the whole family must take refuge in the town of Longford. There is something rather amusing as well as touching in Maria's womanly regrets at leaving her new paint and paper to the mercy of the rebels and the French. "My father," she wrote, "has made our little rooms so nice for us; they are all fresh painted and papered. 0 rebels! 0 French! spare them! We have never injured you, and all we wish is to see everybody as happy as ourselves. " After the family and household had made good their departure from Edgeworthstown, Mr. Edgeworth remembered that he had left, on the table of his study, a list of the names of the men serving in his corps, on whose fidelity he could depend. If this list fell into the hands of the enemy, the men whose names were upon it would probably be selected for bitter and cruel vengeance. "It would serve," wrote Miss Edgeworth, "to point out their houses for pillage and their families for destruction. My father turned his horse instantly, and galloped back. The time of his absence appeared immeasurably long, but he returned safely, after having destroyed the dangerous paper." Even if Mr. Edgeworth did spoil Maria's romances, he must be forgiven for the sake of this act of unselfish gallantry. When the family arrived in safety at Longford, dangers began to arise from another source. It was discovered in the course of a few days that Edgeworthstown House had been left by the rebels entirely uninjured. The corps of infantry which Mr. Edgeworth had brought with him into Longford consisted partly of Catholics. Mr. Edgeworth entertained and defended with vigour a plan for the defence of the town different from that favoured by other persons in authority. All these circumstances were put together with the speed of wild-fire, and created in the minds of the ultra-Protestants of Longford the conviction that Mr. Edgeworth was in secret league with the rebels; this, they were convinced, was the reason why his house had been spared, why he had admitted Papists into any of the bonds of good fellowship; and his plan for the defence of the gaol and the garrison was, they believed, only a trick for making them over into the enemy's hands. Two farthing candles, by the light of which Mr. Edgeworth had read the paper the previous evening, near the fortifications of the gaol, were speedily exaggerated into a statement that the gaol had been illuminated as a signal to the enemy. An armed mob assembled, fully determined to tear him to pieces. He escaped through the merest accident. Seeing him accompanied by English officers ill uniform, his enemies thought he was being brought back a prisoner, and were for the moment satisfied. The incident is illustrative of the conflicting passions which, for so many years, have formed the great social and political difficulty in Ireland.

The rebels and their French allies were defeated at the battle of Ballynamuck, and the quiet family life at Edgeworthstown was resumed. All through the turmoil of wars and rumours of wars, the even tenor of Maria's way was very little disturbed. "I am going on in the old way," she wrote, "writing stories. I cannot be a captain of dragoons, and sitting with my hands before me would not make any of us one degree safer."

Maria and her father had published their joint book, *Practical Education,* in the very year (1798) of the exciting events just narrated. Elizabeth, the second step-mother, also had a hand in it; to her notes, we are told, may be traced the chapter on "Obedience." In this chapter the original view is put forward that in order to form and firmly implant in little children the habit of obedience, their parents should be careful at first only to tell them to do what they like doing. The habit of unquestioning obedience thus formed will, it is thought, be sufficiently strong to bear the strain, when the time comes that the child is told to do things which it would rather not do. There is a considerable element of good sense in this method, as most people will agree who have tried it in the training and teaching of dogs. A much more doubtful theory put forward in the book is that children never should be in the society of servants. This appears to us, in these more democratic days, to savour very much of pride and conceit. It is quite true that parents cannot depute to a hired servant, however faithful, the responsibility of their own position. But to say that a child is on no account to speak to a servant, or to be spoken to by one, appears to us now as most unreasonable and mischievous. How valuable in bridging over the gulf that still separates class from class is the warm affection that often exists between children and their nurses! Many a nurse has vied with a mother in warm and self-sacrificing devotion for her little charges; and all this wholesome and healing affection would be lost if the plan advocated by the Edgeworths were carried out. It is satisfactory to hear that

Mrs. Barbauld protested against this doctrine, and told Mr. Edgeworth that, besides the fact that it would foster pride and ingratitude, "one and twenty other good reasons could be alleged against it." It may be hoped that Mr. Edgeworth acknowledged himself vanquished before this formidable battery opened fire.

One of the most delightful incidents of Miss Edgeworth's later life was her friendship with Sir Walter Scott. When the first of the Waverley Novels appeared, the secret of its authorship had been so carefully kept that every one was in the dark on the subject. The publishers had sent a copy to Miss Edgeworth and her father. As soon as Mr. Edgeworth had finished reading it, he exclaimed, "Aut Scotus, aut Diabolus," *i.e.* "either Scott or the Devil"; and Maria put these words at the top of the letter which she wrote thanking the publishers for the book. Scott was already known to the world by his poems, and to this must be attributed the ready wit of the good guess made by the Edgeworthsfor up to this time neither father nor daughter had had the pleasure of meeting Scott. In 1823, however, they did meet, and the acquaintance soon ripened into a lifelong friendship. Scott acted as guide to Miss Edgeworth and her sisters in showing them the beauties and monuments of Edinburgh. They visited him at Abbotsford, and took a little tour together in the beautiful scenery of the Highlands. There are delightful descriptions in Miss Edgeworth's letters of Scott and his wife; and we have a pretty little picture of Scott and Lady Scott driving out, he with his dog, Spicer, in his lap, and she with her dog, Ourisk, in hers.

When Maria arrived at Abbotsford, and was received by her host at his archway, she exclaimed, "Everything about you is exactly what one ought to have had wit enough to dream." Two years later, Scott, accompanied by his daughter and other members of his family, paid a return visit to Edgeworthstown House. Lockhart, Scott's biographer and son-in-law, was one of the party. In his *Life of Scott* he tells how on one occasion he himself let fall some remark that poets and novelists probably regarded the whole of human life simply as providing them with the materials for their art. "A soft and pensive shade came over Scott's face as he said, 'I fear you have some very young ideas in your head. Are you not too apt to measure things by some reference to literature, to disbelieve that anybody can be worth much care, who has no knowledge of that sort of thing, or taste for it / God help us! What a poor world this would be if that were the true doctrine! I have read books enough, and observed and conversed with enough of eminent and splendidly cultivated minds, too, in my time; but I assure you I have heard higher sentiments from the lips of poor uneducated men and women, when exerting the spirit of severe yet gentle heroism under difficulties and afflictions, or speaking their simple thoughts as to circumstances in the lot of friends and neighbours, than I ever yet met with out of the pages of the Bible. We shall never learn to feel and respect our true calling and destiny, unless we have taught ourselves to consider everything as moonshine, compared with the education of the heart' Maria did not listen to this without some water in her eyes... but she brushed her tears gaily aside, and said, 'You see how it is. Dean Swift said he had written his books in order that people might learn to treat him like a great lord. Sir Walter writes his in order that he may be able to treat his people as a great lord ought to do.'"

The delightful friendship between the two authors continued without interruption till Scott's death in the autumn of 1832. The clouds that overshadowed his later years were bitterly lamented by Maria. She wrote of the "poignant anguish" she felt from the thought that such a life had been shortened by care and trouble. She declined, with one exception, to allow Scott's letters to herself to be published. If they are still in existence, the reasons which caused her to withhold them no longer exist, and judging from all we know of Scott and of her, it would be a great gain to the public to be afforded the opportunity of reading them.

Those who have read this series of short biographies will find a great many of the subjects of these sketches among Miss Edgeworth's friends. She gives a delightful description of Mrs. Fry, whom she once accompanied to Newgate. "She opened the Bible," wrote Miss Edgeworth, "and read in the most sweetly solemn, sedate voice I ever heard, slowly and distinctly, without anything in the manner that would detract attention from the matter." The Herschels and Mrs. Somerville were also numbered among her friends. People sometimes seem to think that women who can write books, and have learnt to understand the wonders of science, will probably cease to care for feminine nicety in dress. It is therefore very pleasant to find that Mrs. Somerville, the author of *The Connection of the Physical Sciences,* and Miss Edgeworth had a conference about a blue crepe turban.

Maria Edgeworth's life did not pass without the romance of love. She received an offer of marriage from a Swedish gentleman, while she was staying in Paris with her family in 1803. She returned his affection, hut refused to marry him, sacrificing herself and him to what she believed to be her duty to her father and family. Her third and last stepmother wrote that for years "the unexpected mention of his name, or even that of Sweden, in a book or newspaper, always moved her so much that the words and lines in the page became a mass of confusion before her eyes, and her voice lost all power." Her suitor, M. Edelcrantz, never married. At the altar of filial piety she sacrificed much.

Nothing is more charming, in the character of Maria Edgeworth, than the sweetness with which she put her own feelings on one side, and welcomed one after another, her numerous step-mothers. The third and last, a Miss Beaufort, was considerably younger than Maria. The marriage with Mrs. Edgeworth No. 4 took place about six months after the death of Mrs. Edgeworth No. 3. No wonder that even the inexhaustible patience of the good daughter was rather tried by this rapidity. She owns that when she first heard of the attachment, she did not wish for the marriage; but her will was in all respects resolutely turned towards whatever would promote her father's happiness. She did not permit her regret to last, and she welcomed the bride not only with unaffected cordiality, but with sincerest friendship.

Another pleasant characteristic of Maria was the cheery way in which she recognised and bore with the fact that she was the only plain member of her family. There is a nice old sister in *Silas Marnsr* who says to some ladies who had not at all recognised their own want of beauty, "I don't mind being ugly a bit, do you?" Maria was like this, except that she thought she possessed a pre-eminence of ugliness over all other competitors. "Nobody is ugly now," she wrote in 1831, "but myself!" Impartial observers, however, state that the plainness of her features was redeemed by the sweetness and vivacity of her expression, and by the exquisite neatness of her tiny figure.

Many examples could be given of her practical good
M
sense and benevolence. On receiving a legacy of some diamond ornaments, she sold them, and with the proceeds built a market-house for the village in Ireland where she lived. In 1826, nine years after her father's death, she again undertook, this time for her brother, the management of the estates. She exerted herself with characteristic energy to alleviate the sufferings of her country during the terrible year of the Irish famine. She died very suddenly and painlessly, two years later, in the arms of her stepmother, on 22d May 1849, aged eighty-two. Macaulay considered her the second woman in Europe of her time, giving the first place to Madame de Stael. She does not seem to us now so great as this; but a variety of interests centre round her, and she well deserves to be remembered.

XVII QUEEN LOUISA OF PRUSSIA. "Sir, if a state submit
At once, she may be blotted out at once

And swallow'd in the conqueror's chronicle.
Whereas in wars of freedom and defence
The glory and grief of battle won or lost,
Solders a race together —yea—tho' they fail,
The names of those who fought and fell are like
A bank'd-up fire that flashes out again
From century to century, and at last
May lead them on to victory."
"The Cup."—Tennyson.

It is very difficult for us now to go back in imagination to the time, between eighty and ninety years ago, when the whole of Europe was in danger of being crushed under the tyranny and rapacious cruelty of Napoleon Buonaparte.

This miraculous man, with his insatiable ambition, his almost more than human power and less than human unscrupulousness, had raised himself from a comparatively humble station, not only to be Emperor of France, but to be the conqueror of Italy, Spain, Sweden, and Germany. He dreamed that in his person was to be revived the ancient empire of Charlemagne, and that all the nations of Christendom were to be subject to his universal dominion. He crowned himself in the presence of the Pope, in Paris, in 1804, and the year following he had the iron crown of the kings of Lombardy placed on his head at Milan. Not content with the title of Emperor of France, he styled himself Emperor of the West, conceding for a time to the Czar of Russia the title of Emperor of the East.

No combination of the other Powers seemed capable of withstanding his wonderful military genius. Most of all his foes, he hated England; because, to the eternal honour of our country be it remembered, England took the lead in rousing the other nations of Europe to resist him. England was the banker of almost every coalition that was formed against him. She supplied men, armies, and armed ships, where she could, and she supplied money to carry on war against Napoleon everywhere. Our great minister, William Pitt, threw himself and all the wealth and power of England into this great struggle against Napoleon. Again and again he revived the spirit of resistance among the other Powers. The rulers and representatives of other countries allowed themselves to be flattered and bribed and threatened into lending themselves to the objects of Napoleon's inordinate ambition. The Czar consented to meet him on intimate and friendly terms; the Emperor of Austria, notwithstanding the cruel humiliations he had suffered, consented to give his daughter to take the place of the unjustly divorced wife of the Corsican upstart; the less important German princes cringed before him. The hostility of England alone was implacable and unceasing, and what made her even more hated, successful.

There is little doubt that Napoleon fully recognised that England was the main obstacle in the way of the fulfilment of his dream of universal dominion. His most darling project was to crush the power of England, and in 1804-5 he made preparations for the invasion of our country, assembling a vast army at Boulogne for that purpose. So fast did his ambition outrun the bounds of fact and common sense, that he actually had a medal struck to commemorate the conquest of England. On one side was his own head crowned with the laurel wreath of victory; on the other, was a representation of Hercules strangling a giant, with the lying inscription, "Struck in London, 1804." He wrote to the admiral of the French fleet, which was destined about two months later to be completely destroyed by our great Nelson at Trafalgar: "Set out, lose not a moment, bring our united squadron into the Channel and *England is ours."* It was at this moment of supreme suspense and danger that Wordsworth wrote that stirring sonnet to the men of Kent, the words of which vibrated through the nation like a trumpet calL

Vanguard of Liberty, ye men of Kent,
Ye children of a Soil that doth advance
Her haughty brow against the coast of France,
Now is the time to prove your hardiment!
To France be words of invitation sent!
They from their fields can see the countenance
Of your fierce war, may ken the glittering lance,
And hear you shouting forth your brave intent.
Left single, in bold parley, ye, of yore,
Did from the Norman win a gallant wreath;
Confirmed the charters that were yours before;—
No parleying now! in Britain is one breath;
We all are with you now from shore to shore:—
Ye men of Kent, 'tis victory or death!

England's immediate relief from the danger of invasion did not come from Nelson's great victory, but from Pitt once more rousing the powers of Austria and Russia to combine against Napoleon. Pitt insisted, in the spring of 1805, on pain of losing the subsidies promised by England, that Austria should at once declare war upon France; and Napoleon was thereupon obliged to withdraw the forces he had assembled in great numbers at Boulogne to meet the new combination that had been formed against him. It was now a question how strong that combination should be. The two great Powers of Austria and Russia had already joined it; the smaller German princes went, some on this side and some on that. The only important Power that showed indecision at this critical moment was Prussia. The King of Prussia, Frederick William III, was a grand-nephew of Frederick the Great; but he bore no resemblance to that sovereign. He was weak and undecided in character, wishing to strengthen and enlarge his kingdom, but without force of character sufficient to decide on a wise line of conduct and to adhere to it. He and his minister, Haugwitz, cast longing eyes upon Hanover, the Electorate of which was then united with the crown of England. The French had seized Hanover, and the possession of this coveted territory was skilfully dangled by Napoleon before the eyes of the King of Prussia. Frederick William III could not arrive at a decision whether he should serve his own interests best by joining the coalition or by remaining friends with Napoleon. While he was hesitating, Napoleon, with his customary disregard of all law, violated a neutral territory, belonging to the Kingdom of Prussia, by taking his army across it. It was like offering one haid in friendship,'and boxing the ears of your friend with the other. Angry as the whole of Prussia was by the insult thus offered her, she did not bring herself boldly to join the coalition of England, Austria, and Russia against Napoleon. The vacillating character of the King and the intriguing diplomacy of Haugwitz stood in the way; but it must not be supposed that in the general body of the Prussian people there was not a feeling of shame, anger, and resentment at the policy that had been adopted by their Government.

The embodiment of this strong national feeling was found in the person of the beautiful young Queen Louisa, a princess of the House of Mecklenburg-Strelitz. Her character was a complete contrast to that of her husband. She had the decision, vivacity, and high courage which he so much lacked. The two were sincerely devoted to one another; but from the essential differences in their dispositions, they became respectively the heads of the two opposing parties in the State; the party who wished to join the coalition and resist Napoleon, and the party who wished merely to look on and try to reap some advantage from whichever side was favoured by the fortunes of war. It seemed at one time as if the Queen's influence with her husband had prevailed, and that Prussia was going to join the alliance; but just at this time came the news of the first of Napoleon's great victories in this campaign, the capitulation of Ulm, and all the fears of the timid party were renewed. Then came the great catastrophe of Austerlitz; Napoleon's forces had completely crushed the combined armies of Russia and Austria, and Pitt's last supreme effort against Napoleon had failed. Austerlitz is said to have

killed Pitt. He was only fortyseven; but his health had long been feeble, and this last blow to all his hopes was fatal. He died a few weeks after the news reached him, on the 23d January 1806. He attributed the failure of the coalition to the indecision of Prussia. If he was right in this he had a terrible revenge. It is one of the most extraordinary episodes in history that Prussia, which had hesitated to join one of the most powerful alliances that had ever been formed against Napoleon, was destined within a few months to match itself against the conqueror almost single-handed.

Very soon after the battle of Austerlitz the Prussian minister, Haugwitz, waited upon Napoleon and renewed negotiations with him. Napoleon offered Prussia the choice between immediate war, or alliance and the possession of Hanover. A treaty was drawn up accepting the latter alternative; Haugwitz agreed to it, and carried it back to his master for ratification. When the terms of the treaty became known in Berlin, the anger of the patriotic party was unbounded. They felt they were bound by ties of blood and kindred to espouse the cause of their German brethren. They looked upon the proffered bribe of Hanover as hush-money, which was to close their lips from protesting against the oppression of Germany by Napoleon. When Haugwitz returned to Berlin he was treated with marked coldness by the Queen. On receiving the disastrous news of the defeat of Austerlitz, she had called to her side her two elder boys, the younger of whom became the late aged Emperor of Germany, and adjured them to think, from that time forth, only of avenging their unhappy brethren. The King's brothers sympathised with the Queen's views, as tlid also the patriotic statesmen Stein and Hardenburg, and a brave young prince, Louis Ferdinand, the King's cousin. Miss Hudson, who has written a life of Queen Louisa, says in reference to her position at this crisis, "The Queen did not desire or endeavour to take a leading part, but she did not dissemble her feelings and aspirations, and her name was put foremost by popular report, on ac-

count of her superior rank. The Queen did not play any conspicuous part, but she was a constant incentive to the best of the nation to work for their country's deliverance. It was what she was, not what she did, that made her name a watchword for the enemies of Napoleon."

Haugvvitz had never dreamed that his master would refuse to ratify the treaty; but the outburst of popular anger against it had been so marked, and the advantages it offered to Prussia were in fact so small, that the King declined to sign, and demanded modifications. His vacillation had placed him in a cleft stick. If he refused Napoleon's terms, he would have to fight with the victorious French army; if he accepted them, and Hanover with them, he would have to fight with England; for it was not probable that the latter country would calmly allow Hanover to be appropriated by another Power without a struggle. While this was the situation of affairs, the King of Prussia, having sent back the treaty to Napoleon to ask for modifications, one of which was to obtain the consent of England to the cession of Hanover, the news came to all the world that Pitt, the most powerful and the most pertinacious of Napoleon's enemies, was dead. England had lost Nelson and Pitt within a few months. It seemed as if they had been removed to make the pathway of ambition smooth for Napoleon.

Pitt was succeeded in the Ministry by his great rival Fox, the professed admirer of the French Revolution, a man whose measure Napoleon thought he had taken, and whom the Emperor believed he could dupe with fine phrases about universal brotherhood and a union of hearts. Napoleon instantly saw the advantage this change might bring to him. With audacity unparalleled, except by himself, he commenced negotiations with the English Government and offered *them* Hanover, notwithstanding that the ink was hardly dry on the treaty in which he had offered it to Prussia. Napoleon, intent for the moment on this fresh project of pacifying England, received Haugwitz, when he presented his master's modifications of the treaty, with harsh and contemptuous insolence. The conditions of the treaty were made still more onerous than before on Prussia. Napoleon now wanted to force a quarrel between England and Prussia, of which he himself would in any result reap the advantages. He carried on this project for a time so successfully that England did actually declare war against Prussia, but hostilities between them never actually took place, because it became evident that Prussia had only been a cat's paw in the hand of Napoleon. The new treaty which Napoleon returned to Frederick William was so humiliating to Prussia, that Haugwitz did not dare to take it to Berlin himself, but sent it by another hand. The King was so weak and foolish as to sign it, and from that moment Napoleon poured insult after insult upon the unhappy government which had consented to its own slavery. One of his first acts was to insist on the dismissal of Hardenberg, one of the most trusted of the Prussian ministers. Under the pretext of a new Confederation of the Rhine, it became evident that Napoleon meant to entirely alter the whole constitution of Germany without consulting Prussia, or any of the Powers chiefly concerned. The French ambassador had orders to state that "his master no longer recognised the Germanic constitution." Under these new humiliations, the war fever burst out more strongly than ever, all over Prussia, Unequal as the contest was, all that was best in the nation preferred any risk to the humble acceptance of the galling tyranny that oppressed them. The young men in Berlin showed what their feelings were by assembling in crowds outside the house of the French ambassador, and sharpening their swords on his doorstep and window sills. It may very well be believed that Fox, if he had lived, would have carried out Pitt's policy in resisting Napoleon. Already his eyes must have been opened by the perfidious transactions about Hanover; but while the process of disillusion was proceeding, Fox died, in September 1806, a few months after his great rival. Napoleon

stated, in after years, that he considered the death of Fox, at this juncture, was the first great blow his power had received. "Fox's death," he often said at St. Helena, "was one of the fatalities of my career." The English policy of resistance to Napoleon had hardly received more than a temporary check by Fox's accession to office, and when Prussia finally decided on fighting with Napoleon, she was promised assistance both from Russia and England. The struggle, however, took place under cruel disadvantages to the weaker side. Napoleon was at the head of 200,000 veterans confident of victory, and of the irresistible genius of their commander. Moreover, the French army, or a great portion of it, was even then on Prussian soil. It was impossible that the Prussian army could rely on Frederick William, as the French army relied on its great general. The Queen did all she could by joining the army, and living in camp, with her husband, to the very eve of the battle, to encourage the spirit of the troops, and above all to prevent any change of front at the last moment. The most experienced of the Prussian generals begged the Queen to remain with the army. One of them wrote, "Pray say all you can to induce her to remain. I know what I am asking; her presence with us is quite necessary."

The final spark which caused the combustible material to burst into the flame of war, was the cruel murder of the Nuremberg bookseller, Palm, by Napoleon, for selling a pamphlet called, "The Humiliation of Germany." He was decoyed upon neutral territory, and was shot on the 25th August 1806, without even the pretence of a legal trial. Rather more than a month later, Prussia had declared war. Her army was very inferior to that of France. The highest number at which it has been put, even with the Russian auxiliaries, is 60,000. The troops from England did not arrive in time to be of any use. In two great battles, Jena and Auerstadt, fought on the same day, 16th October 1806, the power and independence of Prussia were completely crushed. No wonder that all the world at that moment thought them an-

nihilated! A few days later Napoleon made his triumphal entry into Berlin. He occupied the Royal Palaces there and at Potsdam, from which the Queen had lately fled with her children. It was then that Napoleon covered himself with everlasting infamy by a series of bulletins published in an official gazette called *The Telegraph,* in which he poured every kind of insult and calumny upon the person, character, and influence of the Queen. He ransacked her private apartments, read her correspondence, and sought eagerly, but in vain, for evidence to support the monstrous charges he brought against her. She was among the most womanly of women, devoted to her home, to her children and husband. Every true woman is more sensitive on what touches the honour and sanctity of her home than on any other subject. It was here, therefore, that Napoleon struck at her with all the brute violence and perfidy of his nature. M. Lanfrey, the French historian, says that a volume might be filled with all that he wrote and published against her. He wished to render her odious in the eyes of her people, and held her up to ridicule as well as to calumny. He represented that her pretended patriotism was only put on to hide her guilty passion for "the handsome Emperor of Russia," that nothing had aroused her from "the grave occupations of dress, in which she had been hitherto absorbed," but the desire to bring about more frequent opportunities of intercourse with her supposed lover. The stupidity of all this, repeated again and again in bulletin after bulletin, is as wonderful as its wickedness. The effect of it in the minds of the German people is almost as fresh to-day as it was eighty years ago. They had loved and trusted their good, brave Queen, before Napoleon tried to cover her with the mud of his impure imagination. Afterwards, and to this day, they adored her as no modern queen has ever been adored. No stranger can be many days in North Germany now without being forced to ask, "Who is this Queen Louisa, whose portrait is in every shop window, and after whom streets and squares by the dozen are called *!*" Her name has become the symbol of all that is best in German national life, simplicity of living, patriotism and devotion to duty. M. Lanfrey, whose history of Napoleon has been already quoted, says of the bulletins attacking the Queen, "Such circumstances as these indicate the defect of Napoleon's moral organisation, amounting, in fact, to an absence of ordinary intelligence. He outraged the most delicate scruples of the human conscience, because such sentiments had no existence in his own heart. He made a grave mistake in treating other men as if they were as utterly devoid as he was himself of all sentiment of honour and morality. He did not perceive that these base insinuations against a fugitive and disarmed woman, by a man who commanded 500,000 soldiers, would produce an effect exactly contrary to what he intended; that they were calculated not only to excite disgust in all noble minds, but were revolting even to the most vulgar." How little did either the conqueror or the conquered foresee what lay hidden in the womb of time! Prince William, then a delicate child of eight years old, and a fugitive, with his mother, before the victorious army of Napoleon, was destined to become the most powerful sovereign in Europe, to bring to an end the Napoleonic dynasty, and in the chief of the Royal Palaces of France, to be crowned Emperor of a United Germany.

In 1806, however, the fortunes of Queen Louisa and her children were at the lowest ebb. After having lost so much that was more precious than the state and luxury of royalty, the privations of the fugitive Court were not an insupportable trial; the kind peasants brought gifts of money and provisions to their King and Queen, and many acts of faithfulness and devotion cheered and consoled Frederick William and his wife. Even ill-health, which now began to be visible in the Queen, seemed a small misfortune compared with others she had endured. She wrote at this period, June 1807, that her greatest unhappiness was being unable to hope. "Those who have been torn up by the roots... have lost the faculty of hoping."

Still she felt sustained by the confidence that Prussia, though humiliated, was not disgraced. The country had had fearful odds against it, and had been vanquished, but it had striven to do its duty. "Wrong and injustice on our side would have brought me down to the grave," she wrote.

A treaty of peace was now about to be drawn up. Napoleon, the Emperor of Russia, and the King of Prussia, met in a grand ceremonial way at Tilsit. The Emperor of Russia was considered by Napoleon sufficiently powerful to be treated with flattery and consideration. The King of Prussia, being helpless, was harshly dealt with; and when the terms of the peace were discussed, Napoleon was inexorable in insisting on an almost complete destruction of the power of Prussia. All the principal fortified towns in Prussia, including Magdeburg, which commanded the Elbe, were to remain in the hands of the French; and the standing army of Prussia was to be limited to 42,000 men.

The idea appears to have occurred to the Emperor of Russia, that if Queen Louisa joined her husband at Tilsit she could induce Napoleon to modify these harsh conditions of peace. Frederick William concurred, and wrote to the Queen, requesting her immediate presence to intercede with Napoleon for more favourable terms. No wonder, when the King's letter was placed in her hands, that the Queen burst into tears, and said it was the hardest thing she had ever been called upon to bear and do. All her woman's pride revolted against humbling herself to beg for favours from the man who but the other day had so brutally insulted her. But she thought, how could she, who had urged her sons to die for their country, refuse to sacrifice her just and natural resentment for the same end *I* She set out without delay, and the famous interview between herself and Napoleon was speedily arranged. He now treated her with every outward mark of respect, and was perhaps surprised to find the fancy picture he had drawn of her, in his infamous bulletins, falsified in every particular. She would not allow him to tri-

fle with her, and lead the conversation away to commonplaces, but went straight to the object which had brought her to Tilsit, the granting of moderate terms of peace to Prussia. She was calm, dignified, and courteous; once only her self-command failed her: "When she spoke of the Prussian people, and of her husband, she could not restrain her tears." She begged the conqueror at least to grant to Prussia the possession of Magdeburg. The French minister, Talleyrand, who was present at the interview, thought that Napoleon wavered; but a tiger with a kid in his claws does not easily relinquish it, even if an archangel pleads with him. The interview was brought to an end, with no concession promised. The Queen and Emperor met again at a State banquet the same-evening, and again the following day at a smaller private gathering. But she had humbled her pride in vain. Her first words after the final leavetaking were, "I have been cruelly deceived." Napoleon did not hesitate to misrepresent to his wife, the Empress Josephine, the whole bearing of the Queen of Prussia to him: "She is fond of coquetting with me," he wrote; "but do not be jealous." But to Talleyrand, who could not be deceived, because he was present at Tilsit at all the interviews that had taken place between the two, Napoleon said, "I knew that I should see a beautiful woman, and a Queen with dignified manners, but I found the most admirable Queen, and at the same time the most interesting woman I had ever met with." On another occasion he remarked to Talleyrand that the "Queen of Prussia attached too much importance to the dignity of her sex, and to the value of public opinion." From a man of Napoleon's gross and low estimate of womanhood, a greater compliment would be impossible. The French army was withdrawn from Berlin in December 1808. The King and Queen of Prussia did not re-enter their capital till December 1809. In the following July, Louisa died. Spasms of the heart had come on, a short time previously, during the illness of one of her children. They returned with a violence which she had not strength to resist. Her husband and her people felt that she had died of a broken heart. The shorHived rejoicings that had greeted her return to Berlin were now changed into devotion to her memory, and to the cause of German patriotism with which her name will always be associated. The King, his children, and his subjects mourned her loss with unceasing fidelity and reverence. Four years after her death, Frederick William and his Russian allies crushed Napoleon's army at the battle of Leipzig. On his return to Berlin, the King's first thought was to lay the laurel wreath of victory on his wife's tomb. Queen Louisa's eldest son directed that his heart should be buried at the foot of his mother's grave, and the same spot was also selected as the last resting-place of her second son, the Emperor William. It will long be remembered that it was here that the late Emperor, then King William of Prussia/ knelt alone, in silent meditation and stern resolve, on the sixtieth anniversary of his mother's death, just at the time of the outbreak of the war of 1870 between France and Germany.

She was only thirty-five years old when she died; but she was able to leave to her children and to her people a name that will be remembered and honoured as long as the German Empire lasts. Her tomb at Charlottenburg is one of the most beautiful monuments to the memory of the dead, which the world contains. The pure white marble statue of the Queen is by the sculptor Bauch, who knew her well, and honoured her as she deserved. Everything about the building is designed with loving care. The words chosen by-the King, and placed over the entrance of the temple where the monument lies, are: "I am he that liveth, and was dead; and, behold, I am alive for evermore, Amen: and have the keys of hell and of death." XVIII DOROTHY WORDSWORTH

"And were another childhood world my share,
I would be born a little sister there."—
George Eliot.

A Hundred years ago England was particularly rich in great brothers and sisters. There were William and Caroline Herschel, Charles and Mary Lamb, and, perhaps, chief of all, William and Dorothy Wordsworth. These last were certainly the greatest as tested by the position of the brother in the world of literature. He won and maintained a place among the greatest of English poets; but the very greatness of the brother was the cause why the sister is known only as a tributary to his genius. It is not that his achievements dwarf hers by comparison; she made no conscious contribution to literature; she felt from the outset of their life together that he was capable of giving to his countrymen thoughts which the world would not willingly let die, and she deliberately suppressed in herself all cultivation of her own powers, save such as should contribute to support, sustain, and promote his. As Charles Lamb said of his own sister, "If the balance has been against her, it was a noble trade." There is, however, much evidence that the balance was not against Dorothy Wordsworth. She did not sacrifice herself in vain. She chose to give up all independent cultivation of her own considerable poetic gifts, and also to renounce all hopes of love and marriage, for the sake of devoting her whole life to her brother, and of helping to a freer and nobler utterance the poet who has given us "The Ode on the Intimations of Immortality," "The Ode to Duty," "The Happy Warrior," and a host of songs and sonnets among the most beautiful in our language. The sister freely and generously gave, the brother freely and generously received, and freely and generously acknowledged the value of the gift. Over and over again, in prose and verse, Wordsworth acknowledges all that he owes to his sister; never more warmly than when, on the approach of old age, disease had laid its hand upon her, and the long accustomed support seemed likely to be withdrawn. When Coleridge and Dorothy lay prostrate under the stroke of sickness, Wordsworth wrote at the age of sixty-two: "He and my beloved sister are the two beings to whom my intellect is most indebted, and they are now proceeding, as it were, with equal steps, along the path of sickness, I will not say towards the grave; but I trust towards a blessed immortality." If Wordsworth, reviewing the past, could speak thus of his sister, it must be of interest to us to endeavour to discern what her influence over him was, and how their life together was passed.

William Wordsworth was born in 1770, at Cockermouth, in Cumberland, the second son of John Wordsworth, a lawyer and land-agent to the Earls of Lonsdale. Dorothy, her parents' only girl, was twenty months younger than William, and the two children very early showed that close sympathy and tender affection for one another which is often the precious possession of happy family life. Only a few years were spent together by the brother and sister in this joyous playtime of life; but the happiness of this early time is recorded in several of Wordsworth's poems, especially in the one where he speaks of his sister and their visit together to see the sparrow's nest—

She looked at it and seemed to fear it;
Dreading, tho' wishing, to be near it:
Such heart was in her, being then
N
A little Prattler among men.
The Blessing of my later years
Was with me when a boy:
She gave me eyes, she gave me ears;
And humble cares, and delicate fears;
A heart, the fountain of sweet tears;
And love, and thought, and joy.

William and Dorothy were less than nine and seven re spectively when these happy days of childish companionship were closed by the death of their mother in 1778. William was then sent to school, and Dorothy went to live with her maternal grandparents at Penrith. The children were doubly orphaned five years later by the death of their father, in 1783. William and his brothers then passed to the guardianship of their uncles, Richard and Christopher Wordsworth, while Dorothy was made over to the care of other relatives, and spent her time partly at Halifax and partly with her mother's cousin, Dr. Cookson, Canon of Windsor. She and William, however, by no means forgot their childish affection or let it grow cold. They rarely met at this time, but their meetings were looked forward to by both with ardent and intense pleasure. Each continued to be to the other the dearest and most beloved of friends.

Wordsworth, like most generous young people of his day, was deeply stirred by sympathy with the French Revolution. At its outset he believed it would bring immeasurable blessings to mankind; tyranny, cruelty, and vice were, he believed, to be dismissed from the high places of the earth, and in their stead would reign justice, mercy, peace, and love. It is therefore not difficult to imagine with what agony of disappointment he saw, as he thought, all these high hopes falsified, and the light that had been lit by the Revolution quenched in blood and in a series of massacres more cruel and remorseless than any that had disgraced previous forms of government. For a time the belief in goodness and righteousness seemed shaken in him. To disbelieve in the power of goodness is infidelity; and from this gulf of infidelity Wordsworth was saved by his sister's influence. This was the first memorable service she rendered to his moral nature. He was saved from becoming permanently soured and narrowed by the sunny radiance of his sister's sympathy and by her unshaken faith that good is stronger than evil. The brother and sister now resolved to live together; and from that hour Dorothy's whole life was given to enrich and solace that of her brother, and to help him to give utterance to those great thoughts and words which at last made the whole of England aware that the nation was possessed of another poet.

Wordsworth was now twenty-five years of age; he had passed through his college career at Cambridge and had travelled abroad, and the time had come when it was not unnaturally expected of him that he should settle down to some business or profession that would provide him with an income. Very little had come to the family from inheritance, and parents and guardians are not generally disposed to look with lenient indulgence on a penniless young man of

twenty-five who shows a disinclination to any steady work, and is suspected of an ambition to become a poet. Wordsworth's uncles had been kind and generous guardians, but they could not have been pleased at what must have seemed to them at this time the dilatory, desultory life of their nephew. His sister, however, all the while gave him her wannest sympathy and support. Before any one else had dreamed of it, she recognised her brother's genius; she not only believed that he would be a poet, but *knew* that he *was* a poet. She did not urge him, as a wellintentioned but less perceptive friend might have done, to become a lawyer, or a doctor, or what not; she made it possible, by joining her life to his, and nourishing his genius by the tribute she poured into it from her own, that he should have the quiet sympathetic surroundings without which his poetic imagination could not work.

Their slender means were augmented about this time by a legacy which rendered it possible for the brother and sister to have a little cottage home together. Here, at Racedown, in Dorsetshire, Wordsworth first began seriously to devote himself to poetry. Their means were so small that the utmost economy was necessary; but Dorothy cheerfully undertook all the household work of cleaning, cooking, making, and mending. She was not one of those who think there is any degradation, either to man or woman, in manual labour. While she was busied with household cares, her brother often worked in their garden; when their digging and cooking were accomplished, they read Italian authors together, or took long walks through the beautiful country in which they had fixed their abode. It must not be thought that Miss Wordsworth was nothing more to her brother than an energetic, economical housekeeper; she was in feeling almost as much a poet as he was. She had the same intense sympathy with nature, the same observant eye and loving heart for all the various moods of the beautiful outside world. She had also much of her brother's power of expression, and the same felicity in description. It has been said of her, "Her

journals are Wordsworth in prose, just as his poems are Dorothy in verse." Wordsworth said of his brother John that he was " a silent poet," and "a poet in everything but words," meaning that he was a poet in feeling and sympathy; but something more than this can be said of Dorothy; she was a prose poet, who might have become a true poet, if she had not felt that she had another vocation. She was her brother's inspirer and critic, and what she wrote herself proves that she was worthy to be both. Some passages of her diary are almost identical in thought and observation with subjects that Wordsworth has crystallised in immortal verse. On 30th July 1802 we have, for example, in the prose of Dorothy's journal, part of what Wordsworth has given to us in the sonnets on Westminster Bridge and Calais sands. "Left London between five and six o'clock of the morning, outside the Dover coach. A beautiful morning. The City, St. Paul's, with the river, a multitude of little boats, made a beautiful sight as we crossed Westminster Bridge; the houses not overhung by their clouds of smoke, were spread out endlessly; yet the sun shone so brightly, with such a pure light, that there was something like the purity of one of Nature's own grand spectacles. Arrived at Calais at four in the morning of 31st July. Delightful walks in the evenings, seeing far off in the west the coast of England like a cloud, crested with Dover Castle, the evening star, and the glory of the sky. The reflections in the water were more beautiful than the sky itself; purple waves brighter than precious stones for ever melting away on the sands." Whoever will compare this with the two sonnets beginning "Earth has not anything to show more fair," and "Fair star of evening, splendour of the West," will see how far it is just to say that Dorothy has given us in prose what Wordsworth has given us in verse. There is a deeper human passion in Wordsworth's verse than Dorothy ever reached in her prose. He would not stand to-day the third in the noble group where Shakespeare and Milton are first and second, if he had not possessed, over and above his subtle sympathy with Nature, sympathy also with the greatest of Nature's works, "man, the heart of man, and human life." In the "Lines composed a few miles above Tintern Abbey," and again in the "Ode on the Intimations of Immortality," Wordsworth speaks of the change which had gradually come in himself from the days when the worship of external nature, "meadow, grove, and stream, the earth and every common sight," was all in all to him, to the time when— I have learn'd

To look on nature, not as in the hour
Of thoughtless youth; but hearing oftentimes
The still, sad music of humanity,
Nor harsh nor grating, though of ample power
To chasten and subdue.

It was here, as it seems, that his sister could not follow him. Perhaps her self-suppression, the very concentration of her devotion to her brother, closed her powers of receptive sympathy for the wider issues of human destiny which inspires the most precious of Wordsworth's verse. Whether this be so or not, he saw in her what he once had been and had ceased to be.

I cannot paint
What then I was. The sounding cataract
Haunted me like a passion: the tall rock,
The mountain, and the deep and gloomy wood,
Their colours and their forms, were then to me
An appetite; a feeling and a love,
That had no need of a remoter charm.
That time is past,
And all its aching joys are now no more,
And all its dizzy raptures.
For thou art with me here upon the banks
Of this fair river; thou my dearest Friend,
My dear, dear Friend, and in thy voice I catch
The language of my former heart, and read
My former pleasures in the shooting lights
Of thy wild eyes. Oh! yet a little while
May I behold in thee what I was once,

My dear, dear Sister!

After Racedown the next residence of Wordsworth and his sister was (1797) at Alfoxden, in Somersetshire. Here they were visited by Coleridge and Lamb, and here the "Ancient Mariner" was composed, chiefly by Coleridge, but with the help and by the stimulus of Wordsworth and Dorothy. It was during their residence here that the "Lines written above Tintern Abbey" were composed and published. Racedown and Alfoxden were temporary resting-places only; Wordsworth and his sister did not make a real home for themselves till they settled in the beautiful lake country of Westmoreland, in 1799. At first they lived in a small cottage, where Dorothy, with the help of one feeble old woman, whom they employed partly out of charity, did all the domestic work. A few years later they removed to the house at Rydal Mount, Grasmere, which will always be associated with their memory, and where the rest of their lives was passed. It has been pointed out by Mr. Matthew Arnold that almost all Wordsworth's best work was produced in the ten years between 1798 and 1808. During this time he had achieved no fame; he had gained no audience, as it were, save the very select group of whom the chief members were his sister, Coleridge, and Charles and Mary Lamb. All through this time of the production of Wordsworth's best work, Dorothy continued to devote herself to him by the cheerful performance of the double duties of domestic drudge and literary companion and critic. She was also his comrade in many long mountain excursions, in which they both delighted. Miss Wordsworth had extraordinary physical strength, which many persons believe she overtaxed by her long walks over moor and mountain. It is certain, however, that her brother delighted in her physical vigour no less than in her mental gifts. He speaks in lines addressed to her of her being "healthy as a shepherd boy," and in other places he often shows that physical feebleness formed no part of his conception of feminine grace. His ideal woman is ruddy, fleet and strong,

And down the rocks can leap along
Like rivulets in May.

Or again—

She shall be sportive as the fawn,
That wild with glee across the lawn
Or up the mountain springs.

In 1802 the poet married his cousin, Mary Hutchinson, and nothing is more characteristic of Dorothy's sweet and generous nature than the warm, loving welcome which she gave to her brother's wife. She did not know jealousy in love; her love was so perfect that she rejoiced in every addition to her brother's happiness, and did not, as a meaner woman might have done, wish his heart to be vacant of all affection save what he felt for herself. The poet's wife was worthy of such a husband and sister-in-law, and the family life went on in perfect love and harmony, that were only strengthened by the new ties and interests that marriage brought. Wordsworth's children became as dear to Dorothy as if they had been her own, and she devoted herself to them so that they learnt to feel that they had in her almost a second mother.

In 1832, Wordsworth then being sixty-two years old and his sister over sixty, Dorothy's health seriously broke down. So much has been said in some of the books about the poet and his sister of the harm resulting to Miss Wordsworth's health from her long walks, that it might have been imagined that she had been the victim of a very premature decline of physical powers. Considering, however, that she was descended from parents both of whom had died young, it is at least doubtful whether her failure of health at the age of sixty can be fairly attributed to her pedestrian feats. Her illness in 1832 culminated in a dangerous attack of brain fever, from which she recovered, but with mental and physical powers permanently enfeebled. Her memory was darkened, and her spirits, once so blithe and gay, became clouded and dull. Wordsworth and his wife tended her with unceasing devotion. One who knew them well wrote of Wordsworth at this time that "There is always something very touching in his way of speaking of his sister. The tones of his voice become very gentle and solemn, and he ceases to have that flow of expression which is so remarkable in him on all other subjects." The same friend wrote, "Those who know what they (William and Dorothy Wordsworth) were to each other can well understand what it must have been to him to see that soul of life and light obscured."

Notwithstanding the delicate health from which she suffered before the close of her life, she outlived her brother for five years. He died on 23d April 1850, the anniversary of Shakespeare's birth and death. His sister at first could hardly comprehend her loss; but when at last she understood that her heart's best treasure was no more, she exclaimed that there was nothing left worth living for. It was hardly life to live without him to whom her own life had been devoted. The friends surrounding her dreaded the shock which this great loss would be to her, but she bore it with unexpected calmness. A friend wrote, "She is drawn about as usual in her chair. She was heard to say as she passed the door where the body lay, '0 Death, where is thy sting *1* 0 grave, where is thy victory *1* '" She died in January 1855, and was buried by her brother's side in Grasmere Churchyard.

SISTER DORA

One of the most remarkable women who, in recent times, have devoted themselves to nursing and to the service of the sick poor, was Dorothy Wyndlaw Pattison, more generally known by the name of Sister Dora. She was a lady born and bred, well-educated, high-spirited, sweettempered, and handsome; full of fun and sense of humour, fond of hunting and other athletic exercises, and remarkably fond of her own way. As her own way was generally a good way, she was probably right in preferring it to the ways of other people. Strong determination, when it does not degenerate into stupid obstinacy, is one of the most useful qualities any human being can have. In Sister Dora's case her strong will was a great secret of her success, but it also, in a few instances, led her into errors, which will easily be seen as

the story of her life is told.

She was born, in 1832, at Hauxwell, in Yorkshire, a small village on the slope of a hill, looking towards the moors and Wensleydale. Her father was the clergyman of the village, and one of her brothers was the Rev. Mark Pattison, the well-known scholar and the Rector of Lincoln College, Oxford. Dorothy Pattison was first roused to wish for something more than the ordinary occupations of a young lady's life by the enthusiasm felt throughout England in 1856 for Miss Florence Nightingale's work in the Crimea. Dorothy wished to join Miss Nightingale's band of lady nurses at the seat of war, but her parents' opposition and her own want of training prevented her from carrying out this wish. From this time, however, she fretted against the life of comparative inactivity to which she was restricted so long as she remained in her village home. Some years were passed (wasted, we well may think) in unnecessary friction between herself and her father, she desiring to leave home, and he opposing her wishes in this respect. At last she did leave, in 1861, more or less in face of her father's opposition; he declined to make her any allowance beyond what he had been accustomed to give her for pocket-money and clothes, and she had therefore to live partly on what she was able to earn. She obtained work as a village schoolmistress at Little Woolston, near Bletchley, and lived for three years in a small cottage, quite alone, without even a servant; her life at this time must have been very much like that described in *Jane Eyre,* where the heroine gains her livelihood for a time by similar work. She showed, as a village schoolmistress, that keen sympathy with children and power over them which always distinguished her. She could enter, through her bright imagination, into tha feelings and thoughts of children, and her playfulness and love of fun made her a real friend and companion to them. At Little Woolston, too, she did a good deal of amateur nursing for the parents and friends of her little pupils. Her biographer, Miss Lonsdale, says that the people in the neighbour-

hood of the village were very quick to discover that the new schoolmistress was a real lady, but for some time they could not get over their astonishment if they found Miss Pattison blacking her own grate when they came to see her. She was, perhaps, the first instance they had come across of a cultivated woman who thought that "being a lady" was not inconsistent with working hard. Dirtiness, untidiness, and muddle vex the soul of the "real lady" far more than doing the work which produces cleanliness and order.

Sister Dora: a Biography. By Margaret Lonsdale.

After three years at Little Woolston, Miss Pattison made what many must think was the great mistake of her life. Her strong will has already been spoken of; she had found by experience that she could not submit it even to the control of her own father, to whom she was naturally bound by strong feelings of affection. It was necessary to her to have freedom and scope for her energies, and to learn by self-government what she had failed to learn through the government of others. Notwithstanding the incompatibility of her nature with the absolute submission required in such institutions, Miss Pattison joined a High Church Sisterhood, at Coatham, called the Sisterhood of the Good Samaritan. It was part of the discipline of the sisterhood to require unquestioning obedience to all commands. The reason, the feelings, the natural piety of the novices were completely subordinated to obedience as their first and paramount duty. By way of training in unquestioning obedience, Sister Dora, as she was now called, was subjected to various tests of submissiveness; one day, for instance, after she had made all the beds, they were pulled to pieces again by the order of the Superior, and she was told to make them again. In some institutions of this kind, after the floor has been carefully and thoroughly scrubbed by a novice, some one enters, by order of the Superior, with mud or ashes, and purposely makes it dirty again; the novice is then ordered to return to her work and scrub the floor once more, and she is expected to do so without showing the least sign of disappointment or annoyance. It may be true that this system fosters the habit of unquestioning obedience, but if so it must be at the expense of other and more valuable qualities. This unnatural system is perverting to the moral sense and judgment, as Sister Dora, a few years later, found to her cost.

In 1865 she was sent by the sisterhood to Walsall, to take part in the nursing in a small cottage hospital. Towards the end of the year she received orders from the sisterhood to leave this work and take work as a nurse in a private case in the South of England. Walsall had not been trained to habits of unquestioning obedience; its inhabitants and the managers of the little hospital had already discovered Sister Dora's fine qualities as a nurse. They resisted the order that would have deprived them of her services. While negotiations on this subject were proceeding between the Walsall people and the sisterhood at Coatham, news reached Miss Pattison from Hauxwell, to say that her father was dangerously ill and much desired to see her. She telegraphed to the sisterhood, telling them of her father's serious illness, and asking permission to visit him. The answer, which was returned almost immediately, was a blank refusal, and she was bidden to proceed at once to Devonshire to nurse a stranger. Incredible as this may seem, it is still more incredible that the order was obeyed. Miss Pattison had not escaped the paralysis of moral sense which this cast-iron system produces; she turned her back on her home and proceeded to Devonshire. Her father died almost immediately, without ever seeing his daughter again. The shock of this event roused Sister Dora from the lethargy from which she had suffered. She was almost broken-hearted, and deeply resented the dictation to which she had been subjected. She ought to have seen, and probably did see, that the will, like all other powers of the mind and body, with which each one of us is endowed, is given to us to be used; we are responsible for its right

use, and when we use it wrongly, as she did in this case (for it must have needed a very strong effort of will to resist the appeal of love and duty), it is we ourselves who must bear the punishment and endure the anguish of our fault. She did not immediately sever her connection with the sisterhood, but she began from that time to be less completely in thraldom to it. She finally quitted it in 1875, under circumstances which have not been made public. When a friend questioned her as to the cause, Sister Dora's only reply was, "I am a woman, and not a piece of furniture."

After her father's death, Sister Dora returned to Walsall, and in this place practically the whole of the rest of her life was devoted to the service of the sick and of all who were desolate and oppressed. She plunged into her work with all the greater eagerness from her desire to forget herself and the many inward troubles and anxieties which oppressed her at this time. Her great desire was to become a first-rate surgical nurse. Walsall has been described by those who lived there as "one of the smokiest dens of the Black Country," and the workers in the various factories of the locality were often frightfully injured by accidents with the machinery, or by burns and scalds. Sister Dora became marvellously skilful in what is known as "conservative surgery," that is, the art of saving a maimed and crushed limb instead of cutting it off. A good old doctor at the hospital taught her all he knew; but she outgrew his instructions, and Miss Lonsdale gives an instance of a case in which Sister Dora saved a man's right arm from amputation, in spite of the doctor's strongly expressed opinion that the man would die unless his arm were taken off immediately. The arm was frightfully torn and twisted; the doctor said it must be taken off, or mortification would set in. Sister Dora said she could save the arm, and the man's life too. The patient was appealed to, and of the two risks he chose the one offered by the Sister. The doctor did not fail, proud as he was of his pupil, to remind her that the responsibility of what he considered the patient's

certain death would be on her head. She accepted the responsibility, and devoted herself to her patient almost night and day for three weeks, with the result that the arm was saved. The doctor was the first generously to acknowledge her triumph, and he brought the rest of his medical colleagues to see what Sister Dora had done. The patient's gratitude was unbounded; he often revisited the hospital simply to inquire for Sister Dora. He was known in the neighbourhood as "Sister's Arm." During an illness she had, this man used to walk every Sunday morning eleven miles to the hospital to inquire for her. He would say, "How's Sister I" and on receiving a reply would add, "Tell her it's *her arm* that rang the bell," and walk back again. Sister Dora used to say when speaking of her period of suspense and anxiety in this case, "How I prayed over that arm!"

She was particularly skilful in her treatment of burns; sometimes she would take two poor little burnt or scalded babies to sleep in her own room. Those who have had experience in the surgical wards of hospitals know what an overpowering and sickening smell proceeds from burnt flesh. Sister Dora never seemed for a moment to think of herself or of what was disagreeable and disgusting in such cases as these. In one frightful accident in which eleven poor men were so badly burned that they resembled charred logs of wood more than human beings, nearly all the doctors and nurses became sick and faint a few minutes after they entered the ward where the sufferers lay, and were obliged to leave. Among the nurses Sister Dora alone remained at her post, and never ceased night or day for ten days to do all that human skill could suggest to alleviate the sufferings of the poor victims. Some died almost immediately, some lingered for a week or ten days; only two ultimately recovered. Her wonderful courage was shown not only in her readiness to accept responsibility, but in the way in which she was able to keep up her own spirits, and to raise the spirits of the patients through such a time of trial as this. She would laugh and joke, and tell the sick folks stories, or do anything that would help them to while away the time and bear their sufferings with fortitude and courage. She made her patients feel how much she cared for them, and that all she did for them was a pleasure, not a trouble. She used to provide them with a little bell, which she told them to ring when they wanted her. One poor man was reproached by the other patients for ringing his bell so often, especially as when Sister Dora arrived and asked him what he wanted, he not infrequently answered that he did not know. But Sister Dora never reproached him for ringing too often. "Never mind," she would say brightly, "for I like to hear it;" and she told him that she often fancied when she was asleep that she heard his little bell, and started up in a hurry to find it was only a dream. She was so gay and bright and pleasant in her ways, giving her patients comical nicknames, and caressing and coaxing them almost as a mother would a sick child, that they regarded her with a deep love and veneration that frequently influenced them for good all the rest of their lives. Twice while she was at Walsall, there were frightful epidemics of small-pox, and on both occasions she showed extraordinary courage and devotion. She did not bear any charm against infection, and in fact generally caught anything that was to be caught in the way of infectious disease. Her courage, therefore, did not proceed from any confidence in her own immunity from danger. She deliberately counted the cost, and resolved to pay it, for the sake of carrying on her work. At the first outbreak of small-pox in Walsall there was no proper hospital accommodation for the patients; and Sister Dora nursed many of them in the overcrowded courts and alleys where they lived. She was called in to one poor man who was dying of a virulent form of the malady known as "blackpox." He was a frightful object: all his friends and relations, except one woman, had forsaken him; when Sister Dora arrived, she found there was only one small piece of candle in the house, so she gave the woman money to go out and buy candles, and other necessaries. The tempta-

tion was too much for the poor woman, who must, after all, have been better than the patient's other relatives and neighbours, for she had stayed with him when they had run away. But when the professional nurse arrived and gave her money, she ran away too, and Sister Dora was left quite alone with the dying man. Just as the one bit of candle flickered out, the poor man, covered as he was with the terrible disease, raised himself in bed and said, "Kiss me, Sister." She did so, and the man sank back; she promised she would not leave him while he was alive, and his last hours were soothed by her presence. She passed hours by his side in total darkness, uncertain whether he were dead or alive; at last the gray light of early dawn came, and she was at liberty. Her promise was fulfilled; the man was dead

At the second outbreak of small-pox at Walsall, hospital accommodation was provided for the patients; and the ambulance, a sort of omnibus fitted up to convey a patient and nurse, was frequently to be seen in the streets. Sister Dora was as strong as she was courageous; she would come to a house where a small-pox patient lay, and say she had "come for" so-and-so. Resistance and excuses were no good; she would take the patient, man or woman, in her arms as easily as she would a baby, and carry the burden down to the ambulance. Her presence cheered the whole town, and prevented the spread of that dastardly panic which sometimes comes over a place which is stricken by disease. An eye-witness described how every one in the town felt new courage at the sight of the ambulance and Sister Dora, "with her jolly face smiling out of the window."

She spent six months at the small-pox hospital in 1875; and for a long time she was practically alone there with the patients; the doctors of course came by day, and three of her old patients constantly visited the hospital for the sake of seeing if they could do anything for her; and there were two nearly helpless old women from the workhouse, who were supposed to do part of the work; but she was absolutely alone as regards

regular skilful assistance in the nursing and other work. The porter did what he could, showing his devotion by getting up early to scrub and clean for her; but he could hardly ever resist the temptation to go off "on the drink" whenever his wages were paid; on these occasions he would absent himself for four and twenty hours at a time. Once when this had happened, and Sister Dora was quite alone, a delirious patient, a tall, powerful man, flung himself out of bed in the middle of the night, and rushed to the door trying to make his escape. "She had no time for hesitation, but at once grappled with him, all covered as he was with the loathsome disease ... she got him back to bed, and held him there by main force till the doctor arrived in the morning."

One of the trials of her work was that the small-pox patients were nearly all "alive" with vermin; added to this was the horror of the all-pervading smell of pox; in a letter to a friend, Sister Dora spoke of this, and said it was impossible to get away from it. "I taste it in my tea!" For months she never had her bonnet on, or went even as far as the gate; and yet she was able to look back on the time she spent in this hospital as one that had been very much blessed to her. With her High Church feelings about Lent, she wrote cheerfully in the letter already quoted, "Is not this a glorious retreat for me in Lent / I can have no idle chatter." In another letter, she wrote, "I am still a prisoner, surrounded by my lepers. I do feel so thankful that I came.... I thank God daily for my life here."

Endless instances might be given of her physical and moral courage; once, when she was in a third-class railway carriage with a lot of rough navvies, who were swearing and using horrible language, she boldly reproved them; they laid hands on her, one of them exclaiming, "Hold your jaw, you fool; do you want your face smashed in /" She remained quite calm, not struggling, although they were holding her down on the seat between them. When the train reached a station, they let her go, and she got out of the carriage, and one of the men begged her pardon, saying, "Shake hands, mum! you're a good plucked one, you are; you were right, and we were wrong." Another time in the hospital, a half-drunken man, flashily dressed, rang the bell in the night, and on the door being opened forced his way into the hall, and demanded a bed. The night nurse on duty was unable to get rid of him, and Sister Dora was summoned. The man reiterated his determination to stay all night, and Sister Dora contented herself with barring his access to the patients by standing erect on the last step of the stairs with her arms spread from the wall to the balusters. The man seated himself opposite to her, the nurse fled shrieking, and the two waited, staring at one another, each hoping the other would be the first to tire of the situation. Presently the man made a rush down the passage towards the kitchen door, but Sister Dora was too quick for him, and by the time he had reached it she was there with her arms spread across it, as on the stairs, to bar his way. She expected he would knock her down, but instead of doing so he muttered some compliment to her courage, and turned on his heel and left the place.

She had a very strong personal influence for good on the poor rough people, both men and women, for whom she worked. Her religion was one more of deeds than of words, and they saw that both in word and deed it was genuine. Many a one has dated a new start in life from the time he came under her care. Sometimes patients, waking in the night, would find her praying by their bedsides, and it touched them deeply to see how sincerely and truly she cared for them. Although she had the hearty sense of fun already alluded to, no man could ever venture on a coarse word or jest in her presence, and she inspired a good "tone" in the wards even when they were occupied by the roughest and poorest. As time went on there was hardly a slum or court in the lowest part of Walsall where she was not known, and hardly a creature in the town that did not feel he owed something to her. Although most of her time was given

to healing bodily troubles, all her patients felt that she cared for something higher in them than their bodies. She joined heartily in several missions that were started with the object of reaching the lowest and most outcast; she would go quite fearlessly at midnight into the haunts of the most degraded men and women of the town, and induce them, for a while at least, to pause and consider what their lives had been given to them for. Once, we are told, when she was on her way to a patient's house at night, she had to pass through one of the worst slums of the town. A man ran out of a notorious publichouse and said, "Sister, you're wanted; they've been fighting, and a man's hurt desperate." Even she hesitated momentarily, and the thought passed through her mind that she might be murdered. But her hesitation did not last sufficiently long to be visible; she followed the man immediately, taking comfort characteristically in the thought, "What does it matter if I am murdered *I"* To her astonishment, as soon as she reached the group of men, brutalised apparently almost below the level of humanity, a way was respectfully made for her, and every hat was taken off as she passed to the side of the wounded man.

But the time was approaching when the hand of death was to be laid upon this wonderful woman in the midst of all her labours. She was only about forty-four years of age, when she discovered that she was stricken by an incurable and terribly painful disease. It was a sign both of her strength and of her weakness that she insisted on keeping this fact absolutely secret. She, who had always been so strong, could not bear to acknowledge that her strength had come to an end. She, who had been so ready to give sympathy, could not bear to accept it. She went on with her work, bearing her pain silently and proudly, and admitting no one to her confidence. In order more completely to conceal her illness, she left Walsall for a time; and those who remained in charge of the hospital did not dream but that her absence was merely temporary. With the knowledge that her days on

earth were numbered, she still went on studying her profession. She attended some of Professor Lister's operations in London in order to become acquainted with his antiseptic process, and she went to the Paris Exhibition especially to study the surgical appliances shown there. Then presently she came back to Walsall, in October 1878. In November of the same year the Mayor opened a new hospital in her name; she was too ill to be present. Up to the last the townspeople could not believe that their "dear lady" was really to be taken from them, especially as her vitality was so strong that she rallied again and again, when those about her thought that the end was near at hand. She never lost her old habit of joking and making fun out of the dismal circumstances of sickness. Her arm, which became terribly swollen and helpless, she nicknamed "Sir Roger," and she laughed at her doctors because she lived longer than they had predicted she would. She quite chuckled over the idea that she had "done the doctor again." Her life was prolonged till 24th December 1878. The grief throughout the district when it was known that death had removed her was overpowering. The veneration and gratitude of the whole town found expression in many schemes for memorials in her honour. The working people wished most of all for a statue of their dear lady. The wish was gratified, through Miss Lonsdale's generous aid, in the autumn of 1886. A pure white marble statue now stands in a central position of the smoky town of Walsall, commemorating the life and labours of one of the best of this generation of Englishwomen. Her work is another illustration of the text, "He that is greatest among you, shall be your servant." MRS. BARBAULD

Anne Letitia Barbauld will probably be more remembered for what she was than for what she did. At a time when women's education was at a very low ebb, and when for a woman to be an authoress was to single herself out for ungenerous sneers, attacks, and insinuations, Mrs. Barbauld did much to raise the social esteem in which literary women were held, and prove in her own person that a popular authoress could be a devoted wife, daughter, and sister.

Mrs. Barbauld's father was the Rev. John Aikin, a Doctor of Divinity, much esteemed in Nonconformist circles for his learning and piety. He was for nearly thirty years the head of a well-known Nonconformist college at Warrington, round which a little knot of learned and good men gathered, who, it is said, did much to raise the tone, intellectually and morally, of English society at a time when Oxford and Cambridge were sunk in the deepest lethargy, and had comparatively no influence for good in any direction. Among the men, whose names afterwards became honourably known, who were connected with the social or educational life of the Warrington Academy, may be mentioned Dr. Priestley, Dr. Enfield, the Rev. Gilbert Wakefield, Howard the philanthropist, and Roscoe the historian. In the midst of a society tempered by such good influences as these, Anne Letitia Aikin grew from girlhood to womanhood. She and her brother, John Aikin, four years younger than herself, were the only children of their parents. She was born at Kibworth, in Leicestershire, on 20th June 1743, where her father had a school before he became the head of the Warrington Academy. Her mother is said to have come to the singular conclusion that a girl brought up in a boys' school must either be a prude or a tomboy, and Mrs. Aikin preferred the former. Judging from a cameo portrait of Mrs. Barbauld, taken at the request of her friend Josiah Wedgwood, she certainly looks as if a good deal of her time had been spent in the enunciation of the words " prunes, prisms, and propriety." But appearances are notoriously deceptive, and there is a nice little story of Mrs. Barbauld's girlhood, which shows that her excellent mother did not succeed in entirely eradicating the tomboy element from her daughter's character. When only fifteen years old, Anne had attracted the affections of a Kibworth farmer, who made a formal application to Dr. Aikin for his daughter's hand. The Doctor, seeing his daughter in the

garden, gave the suitor leave to go and try his fortunes. When she understood the nature of his errand, her embarrassment was very great, for the dilemma presented itself of having to say "No," and yet to spare the feelings of the swain; finding no other way out of the difficulty, she ran up a tree, thus gaining the top of the garden wall, and then, by one spring, the lane on the other side, leaving her discomfited lover to admire her agility and bewail its results.

Anne was from her birth an extraordinarily precocious child. Her mother wrote of her in after years, comparing her with some less wonderful grandchildren, "I once, indeed, knew a little girl who was as eager to learn as her instructors could be to teach her, and who, at two years old, could read sentences and little stories in her *wise book,* roundly, without spelling, and in half a year more could read as well as most women; but I never knew such another, and I believe never shall." Her father shared sufficiently in the prejudices of the period to refuse for a long time to impart to this gifted child any of the classical learning of which he was the master, and in which she ardently desired to share. At length she so far overcame his scruples that she became able to read Latin with facility, and gained some acquaintance with Greek. The fact that her father was a schoolmaster no doubt enabled her to enjoy many opportunities of instruction and education to which the bulk of Englishwomen at that time were complete strangers. At a time when it was thought enough education for most women if they were able to read, "and perhaps to write their names or so," it is not surprising if schoolmasters' daughters enjoyed an advantage in being able at least to pick up the crumbs that fell from the rich man's table.

Anne was thirty years of age before she made her first appearance in print with a volume of verse in 1773; but she appears to have been known as a poet in her own circle of friends a few years earlier than this, as there is a letter in existence from Dr. Priestley, dated 1769, in which he asks permission to send a copy of her poem, called "Corsica," to

Boswell, who was destined to future immortality as the biographer of Dr. Johnson. Her first printed volume was highly successful, and passed through four editions almost immediately. Thus encouraged, Anne and her brother shortly afterwards printed a joint-volume, called *Miscellaneous Pieces in Prose,* which also attracted much attention and commendation. In Rogers's *Table Talk* an anecdote is given about this volume which illustrates the amusing mistakes sometimes arising from joint authorship. The various articles in the book were not signed by their respective authors, and on one occasion Charles James Fox, meeting John Aikin at a dinner party, wished to compliment him on his book. "I particularly admire," he said, "your essay, 'Against Inconsistency in our Expectations.'" "That," replied Aikin, "is my sister's." "I much like," returned Fox, "your essay on Monastic Institutions." "That" answered Aikin, "is also my sister's." Fox thought it best to say no more about the book.

In the same year as that of the publication of this volume of Essays, 1774, Anne Letitia Aikin became the wife of the liev. Eochemont Barbauld, a descendant of a French Protestant family. Mr. Barbauld's father had been chaplain to the Electress of Hesse Cassel, a daughter of George II, and the son had been intended for the Church of England. He had, however, conscientious objections to taking orders in that Church, and joined the Presbyterian body. Miss Aikin was warned before her marriage that her future husband had suffered already from an attack Of insanity, but with Quixotic devotion this only seemed to her an additional reason why she should unite her life with his. Her married life, notwithstanding many good qualities on her husband's part, was one of exceptional trial and loneliness. Mr. Barbauld was liable throughout his life to fits of insanity, which took the form of fierce and uncontrollable fury as often as not directed against his wife. They settled at Palgrave in Suffolk, and opened a boys' school there. Mrs. Barbauld was much urged by her friend Mrs. Montague to open a school for girls, for the purpose of imparting to them, in a regular manner, various branches of science, such as did not then form an ordinary part of women's education. Mrs. Barbauld declined the task, giving various excuses, such as her own want of proficiency in music and dancing, and other feminine accomplishments. It may, however, be not improbable that her real reason was one that could not be avowed, and was to be found in the mental condition of her husband. It must have been a sufficiently severe trial to the strongest nerves to keep a boys' school, and to know that the head master and principal teacher was at any time liable to fits of insane fury; but this would have been even worse, it would have been a fatal objection, in a girls' school. Poor Mrs. Barbauld set herself with pathetic resolution to make the best of the partner and the life she had chosen. She seems immediately to have assumed she would never have any children of her own, for within a year of her marriage she adopted from his birth her nephew Charles, her brother's son. This was the little Charles from whom *The Early Lessons* and *Hymns in Prose* were written. Very few educational books for young children had then been written, and Mrs. Barbauld set herself to supply the deficiency. She discovered from practical experience the sort of books children learn best from, and the kind of paper and type that suited them best. Many of her friends in the literary world thought she was wasting her talents in such employment. Dr. Johnson is recorded in Boswell's life to have spoken very scornfully of what she was doing, and set it all down to her having married a " little Presbyterian parson." It appears, however, in the anecdotes of Johnson, collected by Mrs. Thrale, that though he might have spoken in this way at times, his warm heart did not fail to appreciate the devotion of Mrs. Barbauld's talents to the humble tasks which her marriage had rendered necessary. "Mrs. Barbauld," Mrs. Thrale wrote, "had his best praise, and deserved it; no man was more struck than Mr. Johnson with the voluntary descent from possible splen-

dour to painful duty." She wrote herself in her preface to *The Early Lessons:* "The task is humble, but not mean, for to lay the first stone of a noble building and to plant the first idea in a human mind can be no dishonour to any hand."

The school at Palgrave was successful mainly through Mrs. Barbauld's efforts; among the scholars were reckoned many men of future distinction, such as the first Lord Denman and William Taylor of Norwich. After eleven years of courageous and exhausting work, the school was given up, and Mr. Barbauld undertook the charge of a Presbyterian church at Hampstead. The husband and wife here enjoyed the friendship of Joanna Baillie and her sister, and here some of Mrs. Barbauld's best literary work was done. But the terrible malady which had pursued her husband throughout his life continued to darken their existence. In order to be near her brother, and enjoy the protection and solace of his society, Mrs. Barbauld left Hampstead in 1802, and removed to Stoke Newington, where Dr. Aikin then lived. But Mr. Barbauld's mania continued to increase, and after a sudden attack which he made upon his wife with a dinner knife, it became obvious that he must be put under restraint. The unhappy man put an end to his own life in 1808. After an interval, Mrs. Barbauld resumed her literary work, bringing out an edition of English Novels in 1810. In the following year she brought out a poem, which she called "1811," very strongly tinged with the despondency which she felt regarding public affairs. She had been bred as a Whig, to hope for great things from the measures of emancipation with which that party had always been identified. Her sympathies were rather with the French Revolution than with the long-continued struggle of England against Napoleon. The poem had a tone of gloom and deep melancholy, which perhaps reflected more of the writer's personal despondency than the circumstances justified. It is not a little curious that a passage in it is credited with having suggested Lord Macaulay's famous prophecy that in years to come a New

Zealander "will from a broken arch of Blackfriars Bridge contemplate the ruins of St. Paul's." The poem provoked a coarse and insulting review in the *Quarterly,* with which it is to be regretted that Southey's name is now identified. Murray, the proprietor of the *Review,* is said to have declared that he was more ashamed of that article than of any that had ever appeared in his magazine. Mrs. Barbauld's friends, Miss Edgeworth foremost among them, expressed their indignation and sympathy; a more ungentlemanlike, unjust, and insolent review, Miss Edgeworth said she had never read; and she wrote an inspiriting letter to her friend, concluding with the words, "Write on, shine out, and defy them." But at nearly seventy years of age Mrs. Barbauld was to be excused if she felt that younger and stronger hands must carry on the fight. The poem referred to was not her last literary effort, but it was the last of her writings published during her lifetime. Very little, perhaps, of her work has permanent value; one poem, however, that beginning "Life! I know not what thou art," which was written in extreme old age, will probably live as long as anything in the language. It indicates possibly what she might have done, had it not been for the tragedy of her married life. Of two lines in this poem—

Life, we've been long together,

Through pleasant and through cloudy weather—

Wordsworth declared that, though he was not in the habit of grudging people their good things, he wished he had written those lines. Her mental powers remained clear and vigorous to the end of her long life. When she was past eighty, writing to Miss Edgeworth, she summed up, as it were, the worth of what she knew and did not know. "I find that many things I knew, I have forgotten; many things I *thought* I knew, I find I knew nothing about; some things I know, I have found not worth knowing, and some things I would give—oh! what would one not give to know, are beyond the reach of human ken."

All her life through she laboured with her pen in defence of civil and religious liberty, against the iniquities of the slave trade, and for many other causes which have made life more worth living in England to-day. She died, universally honoured and respected, in 1825, aged eightytwo JOANNA BAILLIE

Mrs. Joanna Baillie, as she was usually called, because, though she was never married, her age and literary reputation were held to entitle her to brevet rank, was a remarkable instance of a writer rapidly rising to the highest pinnacle of fame, and then as rapidly and surely descending almost to the common level of ordinary mortals. But the Scotch woman, with the blood of heroes in her veins, showed herself worthy of her descent, both by the modesty and dignity with which she bore her fame, and by the sweetness and unassuming simplicity with which she bore the loss of it. She was descended from Sir William Wallace, and the fame of this long-past ancestor is perhaps equalled by that of another and a much nearer relative. John Hunter, the great anatomist and physiologist, the founder of the College of Surgeons, was her mother's brother. She therefore might truly feel, not in a figurative sense, that in everything she was "sprung of earth's first blood"; and her double connection with the best and greatest of the heroes of Scotland was probably not without its influence on the development of her mind and character.

She was born at Bothwell, near Glasgow, on the banks of the Clyde, in 1762. In a poem addressed, near the close of her life, to her sister Agnes, she recalls how they had as children— ... paddled barefoot side by side, Among the sunny shallows of the Clyde.

Her father was a minister of the Scotch Church, and afterwards a Professor of Divinity in the University of Glasgow. His death in 1778, and the establishment of his son Matthew in the medical profession in London, caused Mrs. Baillie and her daughters, Joanna and Agnes, to remove there in 1784; and in London practically the rest of the future poetess's long life was spent. Her first work was a volume of verse published anonymously in 1790. The first

of her series of dramas, called *Plays on the Passions,* was published in 1798. These were also published without the author's name. They made an immediate and very widespread impression; and their author was frequently, and by the very best judges, lauded as being equal, if not superior, to Shakespeare. The idea of these dramas, and of those in the successive volumes which appeared in 1802 and 1812, was to delineate a single dominant passion, such as hatred, envy, etc.; and each of the passions thus treated was made the subject first of a tragedy, then of a comedy. The language employed is easy, dignified, and simple: and it is probable that the contrast Joanna Baillie's dramas afforded in this respect to the dramas of the generation closing with the death of Dr. Johnson, was the reason of the great hold which they at once obtained upon the public mind. It is not easy in any other way to account for their extraordinary popularity. The time in which Joanna Baillie lived was one marked by a literary revolution, in which the formal, stilted, and didactic manner was overthrown, and poets and great writers sought to express their thoughts in simple and natural language. The leaders of this literary revolution were Wordsworth and Coleridge. In the great movement identified with their names Joanna Baillie bore a humbler, but a useful and effective part.

When Joanna Baillie's first volume of plays appeared, there was much speculation as to their possible authorship. Samuel Rogers, the banker, poet, and critic, thought that they were written by a man. It seems to have been difficult, at the end of the last century, for the great judges in the literary world to conceive that a poem, worthy of praise, could be of female authorship. Even so late as 1841, a writer in the *Quarterly Beview,* writing upon Joanna Baillie's poetical works, puts the coping-stone upon the praise which he bestows upon her style and diction by saying that they are "masculine." He says, "Let us again express our admiration of the wonderful elasticity and *masculine* force of mind exhibited in this vast collection of dra-

mas;" and in another place the writer says, "The spirit breathing everywhere is a spirit of *manly* purity and moral uprightness." We should say, at the present day, that there is certainly force of mind in Joanna Baillie's dramas, but that it is feminine, not masculine in character, and that the spirit of purity which breathes through them is essentially the womanly spirit. She had particular power and skill in the delineation of female characters, especially those of an unusual degree of elevation and purity. This in itself would have sufficiently betrayed the sex of the writer now when people have had far wider opportunities of judging of the differences between men and women as authors. Thackeray could give us an Ethel Newcome and a Becky Sharp, but women were needed to give us a Dorothea, a Marion Erie, or a Shirley Keeldar. Mrs. Siddons, the great actress, was charmed by the character of Jane de Montfort in Joanna Baillie's Tragedy on Hatred. The play called *Be Montfort* was put upon the stage by John Kemble, the brother of Mrs. Siddons: they both appeared in it. It ran for eleven nights, but it was not successful on the stage. Joanna's complete ignorance of what was requisite for the success of a play upon the stage foredoomed her to failure; the audience was, in the first act, let into the secret upon which the plot of the whole play turned, consequently as the drama proceeded the interest in it, instead of becoming more and more intense, gradually dwindled away, until in the fifth act it had quite evaporated. Mrs. Siddons, whose admiration for the character of Jane de Montfort has been already mentioned, is said to have remarked to the poetess, "Make me some more Jane de Montforts"—a request which does not appear to have been gratified. In all, five of Joanna Baillie's plays were put upon the stage—two of them, called *Constantine and Valeria* and *The Family Legend,* had a considerable degree of success. *The Family Legend* was brought out in Edinburgh in 1809, under the special patronage of Sir Walter Scott, who wrote the prologue of the play. At a later date it was reproduced in London.

The authorship of Joanna Baillie's first volume of plays did not long remain a secret. Sir Walter Scott was the first to make a successful guess as to the personality of the writer; and the discovery led to the formation of a warm friendship between him and Joanna, which only terminated with his life. Many of Scott's most delightful and characteristic letters were written to her. It was perhaps Scott's too generous appreciation of Joanna's powers as a dramatist that led to her plays being so much overrated, as they certainly were when they first appeared. Scott compared her to Shakespeare. Miss Mitford followed suit, saying of her sister-writer, "Her tragedies have a boldness and grasp of mind, a firmness of hand, and resonance of cadence that scarcely seem within the reach of a female writer." Byron made her an exception to his sweeping generalities concerning the female sex, saying, "Woman (save Joanna Baillie) cannot write tragedy."

In 1825 the golden mists which had surrounded the sunrise of her literary life had melted away. Charles Lamb was too keen a critic probably to have been carried away by the stream of fashion at any time; but in the year mentioned, writing to his friend Bernard Barton, he says: "I think you told me your acquaintance with the drama was confined to Shakespeare and Miss Baillie: some read only Milton and Croly. The gap is as from an ananas to a turnip. " Lamb's contemptuous reference measures the rapid fall from the heights of fame which Joanna Baillie endured, and endured without any failure of sweetness and dignity of character.

Joanna Baillie's day as a poetess was of short duration: it is now chiefly as a woman that she charms and helps us. Her house at Hampstead was for many years a meeting-place for those who were most worth meeting, either for talent or goodness; her kindly and gentle influence brought out all that was best in her guests and companions. In Miss Martineau's autobiography she has something to say about nearly all the lions and lionesses of the literary London of her day, and she singles out our po-

etess for special commendation. "There was Joanna Baillie," she writes, "whose serene and gentle life was never troubled by the pains and penalties of vanity; what a charming spectacle was she! Mrs. Barbauld's published correspondence tells of her in 1800, as a 'young lady of Hampstead whom I visited, and who came to Mr. Barbauld's meeting, all the while with as innocent a face as if she had never written a line.' That was two years before I was born. When I met her about thirty years afterwards, there she was, still 'with as innocent a face as if she had never written aline!' And this was after an experience which would have been a bitter trial to an author with a particle of vanity. She had enjoyed a fame almost without parallel, and had outlived it. She had been told every day for years, through every possible channel, that she was second only to Shakespeare, if second; and then she had seen her works drop out of notice, so that, of the generation who grew up before her eyes, not one in a thousand had read a line of her plays; yet was her serenity never disturbed, nor her merry humour in the least dimmed" *Autobiography,* vol. i. p. 385).

This serene and happy temperament accompanied Joanna throughout her long life. She went on writing till past eighty, and lived to the great age of eighty-nine. Her sister Agnes, her inseparable friend and companion, lived to be over a hundred, and preserved her faculties clearly to the end. Joanna Baillie was never ill. The day be r fore her death she expressed a strong desire to die. She went to hed, apparently in her usual health, but was found to be in a state of coma in the morning, and" she died on the afternoon of the same day, 23d February 1851.

XXII HANNAH MORE

Miss Charlotte M. Yonge's charming little biography of Hannah More brings strikingly before us the picture of the authoress of *Coelebs in Search of a Wife,* and also depicts in a way that will not easily be forgotten, some of the more striking contrasts between the present day and the England of eighty or ninety years ago. There are some who

are always inclined to say "the old is better " ; but they must be very curiously constituted who can look back on the social condition of our country at the end of the last century and beginning of this, without being filled with amazement and thankfulness at the improvement that has taken place.

It is not so generally remembered as it ought to be, that the second half of Hannah More's life was devoted to the service of the poor, especially to the spread of some measure of education and civilisation in the then almost savage districts in the neighbourhood of Cheddar, and of the Mendip Hills. Yet even so advanced an educationalist as Hannah More thought that on no account should the poor be taught to write. In a letter to Bishop Beadon, describing her system of instruction for the poor children in the parishes immediately under her care, she says: "They learn on week-days such coarse work as may fit them for servants. *I allow of no writing for the poor.* My object is not to make fanatics, but to train up the lower classes in habits of industry and piety." We cannot have a more apt illustration of the fact that the advanced reformer of one generation may become, by the natural growth of society, the type of what is most exaggeratedly retrograde in the next. It would be very ungenerous and shortsighted on our part to condemn Hannah More for her narrowness of view. She belonged to a day when the farmers in the village, where she sought to establish a Sunday school, begged her to desist because "religion would be the ruin of agriculture, and had done nothing but mischief ever since it had been brought in by the monks at Glastonbury." At another place her educational schemes were so stoutly opposed by all the leading inhabitants that it was impossible to obtain for the school the shelter of any roof, and the children were accordingly assembled to sing a few hymns under an apple-tree. They were soon, however, driven from this shelter by the fears of the owner of the tree, who said he was afraid the hymn singing was "methody," and that " methody " had blighted an apple-tree belonging to his mother!

Even these examples of ignorance and superstition might possibly, however, be matched at the present day. More thoroughly significant of a state of things that is past and gone for ever, is the following incident. "On a Sunday," about the year 1790, "in the midst of morning service the congregations in the Bristol churches were startled by the bell and voice of the crier, proclaiming the reward of a guinea for a poor negro girl who had run away." The idea of property in human beings is one that is now universally abhorrent; but less than a hundred years ago the loss of such property could be cried in the midst of congregations assembled to acknowledge the Fatherhood of God and the brotherhood of humanity, and it was only one here and there among the worshippers who felt the blasphemy and the mockery of the proceeding.

As an illustration of the extreme hardships endured by the poor before the era of steam manufactures had set in, we learn that the difficulty in obtaining clothes was so great that at Brentford, close to London, thrifty parents bought rags by the pound, and made clothing for their children by patching the pieces together. Brushes and combs, it is added, were entirely unknown. It is no exaggeration, therefore, to say that the poorest beggar of the present day can, if he choose, be more luxuriously clad and cared for than the children of the thrifty poor a hundred years ago. The difference in morals is as great as the difference in manners and education. Hannah More heard a charity sermon, in which the preacher, a dignified ecclesiastic, propounded that "the rich and great should be extremely liberal in their charities, because they *were happily exempted from the severer virtues.*" This was the old Papal practice of the sale of indulgences appearing again in a Protestant dress. No wonder, if this was a type of the Gospel that was preached to the rich, that Patty, Hannah's sister, was accustomed to say that she had good hope that the hearts of some of the "rich poor wretches" might be touched by her sister's eloquence.

The change of manners may be illustrated by the following anecdote. Hannah More, in the height of her literary celebrity, was asked to sit next the Bishop of Chester, Dr. Porteous, at dinner, and make him talk. She pressed him to take a little wine. He replied, "I can't drink a *little,* child: therefore I never touch it. Abstinence is easy to me; temperance would be difficult."

These were days when Edmund Spenser was not considered a poet, and when Dryden and Pope were preferred to Shakespeare. Hannah, however, defended Milton's *L'Allegro, Il Penseroso,* and *Lycidas,* against the strictures of Dr. Johnson; though they found themselves in entire agreement in depreciating Milton's sonnets. Johnson's simile for a sonnet was "a bead carved out of a cherry stone." The noble and solemn music of Milton's majestic sonnets certainly did not harmonise with Johnson's image, and, therefore, as Milton's sonnets were not pretty playthings, it was agreed that he could not write sonnets.

The bigotry and narrowness of religious criticism at that' day may be measured by the fact, which Hannah mentions in one of her letters, that her book on *Practical Piety* had been attacked by the Calvinists as giving a sanction to idolatry, because she had spoken of the sun as "he." She did not altogether escape being tarred with the same brush, if we may judge from the passage in *Ccelebs,* where she makes Mr. Stanley complain of Day's *Sandford and Merton,* and other books which had lately been written for the young, that there was "no intimation in them of the corruption of human nature, and thus that they contradict the catechism when it speaks of being 'born in sin, and the children of wrath.'" She could not help, it appears, taking her religion sadly, as English people are supposed to take their pleasures. There was, however, a great fund of natural gaiety and lightheartedness in her, but whether she considered this one of the results of being a child of wrath or not, she did not seem to think gaiety, any more than writing, was a thing to be encouraged in the

poor. She describes a great meeting of the schools founded by herself in the Mendip Hills. This annual "Mendip feast" took the form of what we should now call a gigantic school treat. The schools established were spread over an area of twenty-eight miles, and nearly the whole population of the villages, to the number of seven or eight thousand people, attended. The children were generously regaled on substantial fare. But nothing in the form of a game or a festivity of any kind was permitted. The singing of "God sa/ve the King" "is the only pleasure in the form of a song we ever allow.... The meeting," she says again, "took its rise from religious institutions. The day passed in the exercise of duties, and closed with joy. Nothing of a gay nature was introduced...."

One cannot help thinking, on reading this, that she had only herself to thank if, in spite of all her talents and goodness, her name became a byword for severity and primness. Charles Lamb speaks in one of his early letters of "outHannahing Hannah More"; and she herself tells what she states is a true story, illustrating the way in which she was regarded in circles where childish merriment was not discountenanced: "A lady gave a very great children's ball," wrote Miss Hannah, somewhere about 1792: "at the upper end of the room, in an elevated place, was dressed out a figure to represent me, with a large rod in my hand, prepared to punish such naughty doings."

The pity of this was that her natural disposition seems to have been sprightly and gay enough; her verses and other compositions often show a very pretty wit. If she had been as merry when she undertook her great work on the Mendips, as she was in the days when she was the friend and constant companion of Garrick, Johnson, and Horace Walpole, the general impression left by her character would have been a much more attractive one. Miss Yonge thinks that the chief reason of the austerity of her religion is to be found in the low condition of morals at the time. "There was scarcely," she writes, "an innocent popular song in existence, simple enough,"... "and unconnected with evil, and the children and their parents were still too utterly rough and uncivilised to make it safe to relax the bonds of restraint for a moment." We cannot think that this excuse is altogether valid: the age that had produced "John Gilpin" and "Goody Two Shoes " can hardly be said to be without one innocent popular song or story which would amuse children. The gloomy complexion given to religion by the school of which Hannah More was a member has a great deal to answer for; in some temperaments, among whom the poet Cowper may be quoted as a type, the gentle and sensitive nature was plunged into profound and morbid melancholy which wrecked the whole existence of its victim; in others, of a more energetic and rebellious character, it produced a violent reaction, not only against religion, but against all moral order, and every kind of restraint Just as the excesses of the reign of Charles II. followed the grim and rigid piety of Puritan England, so the orgies of the Prince Regent and his boon companions followed the austere and mirthkilling religion of the early evangelicals. About the time of which we are now writing, a serious attack was made in one of the religious papers upon Jane Taylor, the joint authoress with her sister of *Hymns for Infant Minds,* because in one of her stories she had represented, without reprobation, a family party of young children enjoying a dance together. When people impute wickedness to actions that are in themselves innocent and harmless, they are tampering with and weakening their own moral sense, and that of all those brought within their influence. To invent sins generally ends in manufacturing sinners.

Hannah More, the youngest but one of five sisters, daughters of Jacob More, master of the school at Stapleton, near Bristol, was born about 1745. Her father belonged to a Norfolk family, several members of which had been numbered amongst Cromwell's Ironsides. Jacob More, however, forsook the family traditions both in politics and religion. He became a churchman and a Tory; and

this may have been the cause of his leaving the home of his fathers, and settling in the West Country. He here married a farmer's daughter, of whom little is known except that she persuaded her husband to impart his classical and mathematical learning to his clever little daughter, and that by many acts of motherly sympathy she encouraged her children to use the talents with which Nature had very liberally endowed them. The five sisters, Mary, Betsy, Sally, Hannah, and Patty, were a tribe of whom any mother might have been proud. Hannah and Patty were inseparable, sharing every hope and every occupation and possession. Their taste was for literature. Sally was the wit of the family. Mary and Betsy supplied the practical, housewifely element in the quintet. As a little girl, Hannah's two ambitions were to "live in a cottage too low for a clock, and to go to London to see bishops and booksellers!" At the age of twenty-one, Mary More set up a school on her own account in Bristol. Betsy and Sally were her assistants, and Hannah and Patty were among the first batch of pupils. Sally in after years thus described this adventurous proceeding to her friend Dr. Johnson: "We were born with more desires than guineas. As years increased our appetites the cupboard at home grew too small to gratify them; and with a bottle of water, a bed, and a blanket, we set out to seek our fortunes. We found a great house with nothing in it—and it was like to remain so—till, looking into our knowledge-boxes, we happened to find a little *laming*—a good thing when land is gone, or rather none, and so at last, by giving a little of this laming to those who had none, we got a good store of gold in return" (pp. 6, 7, Miss Yonge's *Hannah More).*

Hannah's unusual abilities soon began to attract notice. She wrote a play for school acting, which had a great success; we are told how on one occasion, when she was ill (her health was always delicate), her doctor was so earned away by the charm of her conversation that he forgot to make any inquiries about her health; he took his leave, and

was on the point of departing from the house, when he returned with the inquiry, "And how are you, my poor child *1"*

Hannah's first visit to London was about 1772 or 1773, when she was twenty-seven or twenty-eight years old. She saw the first performance of Sheridan's *Rivals,* and sagely remarks that the writer must be treated with indulgence, for that "much is to be forgiven in an author of twentythree, whose genius is likely to be his principal inheritance." She was introduced to Miss Reynolds, Sir Joshua's sister, and this lady promised to make her known to Dr. Johnson. She saw Garrick, the great actor, in *King Lear,* and was so much impressed by him that she wrote a long description of his acting in a letter that was handed about among her friends and gained a sort of half publicity, as seems to have been not unusual at that time. This letter paved the way for an introduction to Garrick and his wife, and Hannah More became one of their most intimate and valued friends. Garrick encouraged Hannah to write for the stage, and some of her pieces, under his fostering care, had an astonishing degree of success. Garrick's favourite name for the poetess was "Nine," by way of delicate comparison with the nine muses. Horace Walpole used to call her "Saint Hannah." Dr. Johnson called her "a saucy girl," perhaps the nicest epithet of the three. When Garrick died, Hannah was one of the ladies admitted to Westminster Abbey to witness his funeral. Hannah spent the first year of her friend's widowhood with Mrs. Garrick at her house near Hampton; and on many other occasions it was shown, in a similar way, that Hannah was one on whom her friends were accustomed to depend for sympathy and support in the darkest hours of mourning and sorrow. After Garrick's death Hannah never visited a theatre again. She did not even go to see her own play, *The Fatal Falsehood,* which Garrick had been preparing to put on the stage at the time of his death.

From the time of her first entry into London society she seems to have had access to all that was best in the world of literature and art, and to have played a distinguished part there. It is, therefore, the more to her credit that she turned from this gay and brilliant life in order to devote herself to the work of education and civilisation among the poor people of Cheddar and the Mendips.

She and her sister Patty had settled in a pretty cottage home called Cowslip Green, in the parish of Wrington, Bristol Here they were visited by their friends from the great world, and hence they, in their turn, made their annual visit to London. Mention has already been made of the painful impression produced in Hannah on hearing, in a Bristol church, the loss of a negro girl proclaimed by the crier in the midst of the morning service. She was a woman much influenced by her friendships. She had been a poetess and dramatist under the influence of Johnson and Garrick; Wilberforce and John Newton (Cowper's friend) had now awakened in her a passion of pity for slaves and a passion of hatred against slavery. Miss Yonge states that Hannah was before this a friend of Lady Middleton, "who had first inspired William Wilberforce with the idea of his great work in life; and on going to make her annual visit to Mrs. Garrick in the winter of 1787, she first heard of the Bill that was to be introduced into Parliament for the abolition of slavery." In 1789 William Wilberforce came to spend a few days with the Misses More, at Cowslip Green. By way of showing him the beauties of the neighbourhood the ladies sent him to see the picturesque cliffs and caves of Cheddar. When their guest returned he was remarkably silent; the food that had been sent with him was untasted, and he remained for some hours alone in his room. His hostesses naturally feared that he was ill; but when he rejoined them they discovered that instead of admiring the natural beauties of Cheddar, the tender heart of the future emancipator of the slaves had been wholly engrossed by the evidences which had presented themselves of human depravity, misery, and neglect. The inhabitants of

the picturesque region were almost savages; their poverty was frightful; there was no sort of attempt at education of any kind; there were no resident clergymen; the people were utterly lawless; it was unsafe for a decent person to go amongst them unprotected; writs could not be served but at risk of the constable being thrown down some cliff or pit. These things Wilberforce had discovered, and they obscured for him all the pleasure which pretty scenery could afford. "Miss More," he said, "something must be done for Cheddar;" and after much consultation and thought, before he went away, he again charged the ladies with the task of civilising and educating the wild district which lay at their doors, adding, "If you will be at the trouble, I will be at the expense."

From this time the sisters led a new life. It is true that Hannah did not give up her literary pursuits; she laboured with her pen as well as with other instruments in pursuit of her end. But now the main object of both Patty and Hannah was to educate and reclaim the inhabitants of the districts which have been named. The work, merely from a physical point of view, was by no means light. There were no roads, or such bad ones that the only practical means of travelling was on horseback. Their first task was to endeavour to gain the goodwill and assistance of the farmers and gentry. Patty says of some of these, "They are are as ignorant as the beasts that perish; intoxicated every day before dinner, and plunged into such vice that I begin to think London a virtuous place." Such clergy as did occasionally visit the district might as well have stayed away. Of one Patty says, "Mr. G is intoxicated about six times a week, and very frequently is prevented from preaching by two black eyes, honestly earned by fighting." The sisters showed their good sense, as well as their benevolence, by finding out and utilising whatever in the way of a good influence existed in the district. They rejected no help because the helper did not conform to their particular pattern of orthodoxy. They did not hesitate, although they were strict churchwomen,

to engage a Methodist to act as mistress in one of their Sunday schools. They soon had thirteen villages under their care, and an improvement began to be visible in nearly all of them. Of one of them, Congresbury, Hannah wrote describing the first opening of the school: "It was an affecting sight. Several of the grown-up youths had been tried at the last assizes, three were the children of a person lately condemned to be hanged, many thieves, all ignorant, profane, and vicious beyond belief. Of this banditti we have enlisted one hundred and seventy; and when the clergyman, a hard man, who is also the magistrate, saw these creatures kneeling round us, whom he had seldom seen but to commit or punish in some way, he burst into tears. I can do them little good, I fear, but the grace of God can do all...."

The Misses More did not escape bitter persecution and misrepresentation in their good work. A Mr. Bere, curate of Wedmore, distinguished himself by his furious hostility to them. He threatened them with penal proceedings for teaching without a license, induced the farmers to make formal complaint to the Archdeacon against them, and obtained an affidavit from a half-witted young man, whom they had befriended, making personal charges against them. Influential friends, however, came to the ladies' assistance. The good Bishop said, "When he heard it was Miss Hannah More he knew it was all right." But the persecution they endured was not without its effect on their health and spirits. Hannah was laid up for about two years at this time, and was unable to pursue her work amongst her poor scholars.

In 1802 the sisters removed from Cowslip Green to Barley Wood; here Hannah wrote some of her best known books. None of her works is better known, at least by name, than *Calebs in Search of a Wife.* Here also, by the request of Queen Charlotte, she wrote a book of advice on the education of Princess Charlotte, who, it was thought, was destined to become Queen of England. *The Shepherd of Salisbury Plain* was written at Cowslip Green, as one of a large series of simple stories for the poor, intended by the sisters to counteract and undersell popular literature of an objectionable character. The Misses More produced three of these tracts a month, and it is calculated that more than two millions were sold in a year. By many *The Shepherd of Salisbury Plain* was considered Hannah More's masterpiece. Wilberforce said he "would rather present himself before Heaven with the *Shepherd* in his hand than with *Peveril of the Peak."*

At Barley Wood Hannah experienced the great and unavoidable calamity of old age, the gradual loss, by death, of the friends and allies of her youth. Johnson, Burke, Reynolds, and Garrick were dead long ago, and the brilliant society in London, of which Hannah had formed part, had lost many of its stars. One by one, death laid its hand on the members of the More sisterhood, till Hannah and Patty, the lifelong friends and companions, were the only two left In September 1819, Mr. and Mrs. Wilberforce being on a visit to the sisters, Patty sat up till a late hour of the night talking to her guests of old days, and Hannah's first introduction to London. In the morning the first news that met the visitors' ears was that Patty was dying. She lingered about a week, but never regained consciousness, and then Hannah was left quite alone, the last of all the five. But her friends gathered round her, and her vigorous intellect and strong sense of duty did not allow her to be idle. She still had vivacity enough to write humorous letters and verses, and to poke fun at what she considered the misdirected zeal of some educationalists.

A few years before her death, Hannah More removed to Windsor Terrace, Clifton. Her old age was cheered by the companionship of a friend, Miss Frowd, of whom Miss More wrote, she is "my domestic chaplain, my house apothecary, knitter and lamplighter, missionary to my numerous and learned seminaries, and, without controversy, the queen of clubs" (penny clubs). When an old lady of more than eighty can write in this buoyant strain, it is the more to be regretted that she seemed to have thought gaiety was a thing it was dangerous to encourage a taste for in the poor. Still, though we cannot help regretting this, we shall do well if we can imitate, in however humble a degree, her unselfish devotion to goodness and the way in which she spent the best years of her life in trying to improve the lot of the most destitute and miserable of her neighbours. She lived to be eighty-eight. She had no long illness, and no failure of any of her mental faculties, except that of memory. Her body became gradually weaker, and she longed for death. One day " she stretched out her arms, crying, 'Patty! joy!'" She never spoke again, dying a few hours later, on 7th September 1833.

XXIII THE AMERICAN ABOLITIONISTS PRUDENCE CRANDALL AND LUCRETIA MOTT

Everybody is an Abolitionist now. There is not, probably, in any part of Europe or the United States a single human being who would now defend slavery as an institution, or who thinks that for man to own property in his fellow-man, to be able to buy and sell him and dispose of his whole life, is not a sin and an outrage against all feelings of humanity.

Slavery was put an end to in the British Dominions nearly seventy years ago, but it is only twenty-six years since it was abolished in the United States of America. The time is well within the memory of many persons now living when to be an Abolitionist, even in the New England States, was to be hated and reviled, to render one's self the object of the bitterest persecution, to risk comfort, happiness, and even life. In England the Abolitionist party was headed by men like Wilberforce, Clarkson, Macaulay, and Buxton, who all enjoyed the advantages belonging to education, good social position, and comparative wealth. It was always "respectable" in England to be an Abolitionist, and it was not necessary to possess the courage and devotion of a martyr to declare one's hatred of slavery. But in the United States it was quite otherwise. Great and influential people of all parties there were for many years vehemently opposed to the emancipation of the slaves. Even as late as 1841 Miss Martineau describes the great sensation made among "the *Mite* of intellectual Boston" when they found that Lord Morpeth (afterwards the Earl of Carlisle), who was then on a visit to the United States of America, had openly expressed his sympathy with the principles of the Abolitionists.

In 1835 the Boston mob dragged William Lloyd Garrison, the leader of the American Abolitionists, through the streets with a rope round his neck; and his life was only saved from their fury through the stratagem of the Mayor, who committed him to gaol as a disturber of the peace. In 1841 the feeling against the Abolitionists was a little less violent; but "anti-slavery opinions were at that time in deep disrepute in the United States; they were 'vulgar,' and those who held them were not noticed in society, and were insulted and injured as often as possible by genteeler people and more complaisant republicans." It was a matter of great astonishment to the polite world of Boston that the English aristocrat made no secret of the fact that he shared the opinions of the despised and hated Abolitionists.

In 1828 Garrison was a poor lad, working for his living as a printer; he determined to devote himself to the gigantic task of freeing his country from the curse of slavery. He began to print with his own hands and publish an antislavery paper called the *Liberator.* He wandered up and down the United States as an anti-slavery lecturer; by and by a few friends began to gather round him, and those who shared his principles and his enthusiasm gradually made themselves known to him. In 1833, being then twenty-eight years old, he received a letter from a young Quaker lady, Miss Prudence Crandall, who asked his advice under the following circumstances: Two years previously she had bought a large house at Canterbury, in the State of Connecticut, and had started there a boarding-school for girls. She had flourished beyond her expectations, and had every prospect of forming a highly successful school. She wrote to Garrison and asked his advice about changing her white scholars for coloured ones. She says in her letter, very simply, not giving herself any airs of martyrdom, "I have been for some months past determined, if possible, during the remainder of my life to benefit the people of colour." Under these quiet words lay a firmness of purpose that would have supported her to the stake if need were. She did not, on that occasion, tell Garrison that she had already admitted to her classes, not as a boarder, but as a day scholar, a very respectable young negro woman, whose family she knew well as members of the church which she herself attended. By this action she had given great offence to the "genteel" inhabitants of Canterbury. The wife of an Episcopal clergyman who lived in the town told her that if she retained "that coloured girl" the school would be ruined. Prudence replied, that though the school might be ruined she would not turn her scholar out. She soon discovered that many of her pupils would leave, not to return, if the coloured girl were retained, but this did not shake her resolution. She began to consider whether it would not be possible to have a school for coloured girls only; and upon this point, not saying anything of her own sacrifices, she wrote, as before mentioned, to consult Garrison. Very soon after the date of this letter the *Liberator* newspaper contained an advertisement, stating that " Miss P. Crandall (a white lady), of Canterbury, Conn." had opened a "High School for young coloured ladies and misses."

By this time the town of Canterbury had put itself into the greatest state of excitement about Miss Crandall's project. She might have reasonably thought when she had converted her school into one for "young coloured ladies and misses" only, that so long as she and her pupils and their parents were satisfied no one else had any concern in the matter. But this was not the view taken by the inhabitants of Canterbury. Three town's meetings were summoned in one week to consider what measures could

be taken to stop and thwart her project. At first it seems to

Q have been thought desirable to try the fair means of persuasion, and Miss Crandall was waited on by a deputation of leading gentlemen of the place, who professed to feel " a real regard for the coloured people, and perfect willingness that they should be educated, *provided it could be effected in some other place."* Miss Crandall's scheme of educating them in her own house in Canterbury would, they assured her, bring disgrace and ruin on the whole town. Miss Crandall heard them out, and then announced her determination to carry out her plan. There was an immovable firmness under the tranquillity of the young Quakeress's demeanour. Another town's meeting was called, and Miss Crandall was allowed to be represented by counsel, but the gentlemen who took up her cause were not granted a hearing, on the ground that they were outsiders, not natives of the town, and the whole of Canterbury, in public meeting assembled, then proceeded to vote their unanimous disapprobation of the school, and their fixed determination to oppose it at all hazards. They certainly opposed it with great vigour, but the hazard was not so much to the town of Canterbury as to the young woman, who was the object for two years of the most relentless persecution. She all the while maintained her quiet dignity, causing Garrison to exclaim in a letter to a friend, "Wonderful woman! as undaunted as if she had the whole world on her side! She has opened her school and is resolved to persevere." One of her friends wrote to Garrison: "We shall have a rough time, probably, before the year is out. The struggle will be great, no doubt, but God will redeem the captives.... We are all determined to sustain Miss Crandall if there is law in the land enough to protect her. She is a noble soul!"

The fight between the heroic little Quaker woman and the town of Canterbury soon waxed very hot. Almost directly after the school was opened in 1833, her enemies procured the passing of an Act by the State Legislature of

Connecticut, prohibiting private schools for non-resident coloured persons, and providing for the expulsion of such scholars. The fact is a warning of the way in which small local parliaments may be carried away by local passions. Such an Act would probably, even then, never have passed the Legislature of the United States. As it was, its originators must have been ashamed of it as soon as their rage against Miss Crandall had had time to cool, for it was repealed in 1838; but in the five years during which it was in operation it gave Miss Crandall's enemies great power over her. Under this Act she was twice arrested, tried, convicted, and imprisoned. She appealed to the Supreme Court, and had the satisfaction in the' superior tribunal of defeating her persecutors, though only on a technical point of law. But in the interval she was subjected to the most extraordinary and inhuman persecution. There was not a shopkeeper in the town who would sell her, or any member of her household, a morsel of food; she and her scholars were not admitted to take part in public worship; no public conveyance would take them as passengers; doctors would not attend them. Miss Crandall's own relations and friends were warned that if they valued their own safety they must not visit her or have anything to do with her. "Her well was filled with manure, and water from other sources was refused; the house itself was smeared with filth, assailed with rotten eggs and stones, and finally set on fire." (See *Life of William Lloyd Garrison,* vol. i. p. 321). But the little "school-marm " held her own. Unlike that Frenchman of whom we are told that he consecrated a long life to coming invariably to the assistance of the strongest side, she was emphatically the friend of the oppressed, and one of that band "who through faith subdued kingdoms, wrought righteousness, obtained promises, stopped the mouths of lions, quenched the violence of fire, escaped the edge of the sword, out of weakness were made strong, waxed valiant in fight, turned to flight the armies of the aliens."

The existence of a group of such

women is one of the most precious national possessions of the American people. Miss Crandall, now Mrs. Philleo, is still (1889) alive and in full vigour of mind and body. The revenge which the whirligig of time has brought to her is the triumph of her cause. She now enjoys a small pension granted to her by the Government of the United States in recognition of her services to the anti-slavery cause.

Another of the famous anti-slavery women of the United States was Lucretia Mott. She, too, was a Quakeress, as were a very considerable proportion of the women who first took up the Abolitionist movement. At one time the Puritan inhabitants of New England, who had fled from their homes in Europe to escape persecution, instituted the most cruel persecution against the Quakers and all sects who differed from the Puritan creed. The persecuted are often only too ready to become persecutors in their turn. Lucretia Mott's ancestors, the Coffins, descended from the ancient Devonshire family of that name, had fled before this Puritan persecution to the island of Nantucket to the east of Massachusetts. Here Lucretia was born in 1793, and here her childhood was passed till she was eleven, when her father removed to Boston, Massachusetts. Lucretia and her younger sister, spoken of in her father's letters as "the desirable little Elizabeth," had opportunities of education at Boston that would have been quite out of the question in the primitive island of their birth. At the age of eighteen Lucretia married James Mott, and her home henceforward was at Philadelphia. Partly for the sake of educating her own children, and partly with the view of helping her mother, who had been left a widow with five children to support, Lucretia Mott opened a school. When she was about thirty years of age she began gradually to be drawn into work of a more public kind, through her deep interest in many moral movements of her time. Foremost among these stood the anti-slavery agitation; she travelled many thousands of miles, speaking and lecturing for the anti-slavery cause. It was then, even in

America, quite a novelty for women to take an active part in public movements, and some of the more old-fashioned of the Abolitionists did not approve of the participation of Lucretia Mott and other women in the work. But Garrison was always, from the first, as eager for the equality of women as he was for the emancipation of the slaves; and he felt too deeply what the anti-slavery cause in England and America owed to women to tolerate their being set on one side without any recognition of their work. However, at first only a minority held this view, and the difficulty which some men felt in working with women caused Lucretia Mott to form the Philadelphia Female Anti-Slavery Society. At the first meeting of this society, none of the ladies felt competent themselves to take the chair, so they elected a negro gentleman to that position, a choice which Mrs. Mott explained a few years later in the following words: "Negroes, idiots, and women were in legal documents classed together; so that we were very glad to get one of our own class to come and aid us in forming that society."

In 1840 Lucretia Mott was one of the delegates chosen to represent American societies at the World's Anti-Slavery Convention held in London in that year. It is well known that she and all other lady delegates were refused recognition because they were women. Sir John Bowring, Mr. Ashurst, and Daniel O'Connell were among those who protested against this arbitrary act of exclusion; but the protest was in vain. Garrison had not been present when the question of refusing to allow the lady delegates to take part in the Convention was discussed. He arrived in England five days after the question had been settled. With characteristic generosity, he refused to sit as a delegate where the ladies had been excluded. They had been relegated as spectators to a side gallery, and he insisted on taking his seat there also. The absurdity of holding a World's Anti-Slavery Convention in which the chief workers against slavery were present as spectators, not as participators, caused a great deal of discus-

sion at the time; and the general movement in England towards the social, educational, and political equality of women may be said to date from that period.

For thirty years Lucretia Mott hardly ever let a day pass without doing something to weaken the fabric of slavery, which she felt to be the greatest curse of her native land. Her manner and voice were sweet, solemn, and tranquil; her small and fragile figure, her exquisite womanliness of demeanour, made it difficult to believe that she could become the object of violent hatred and persecution. Yet she had often known what it was to stand on a platform in the midst of a shower of stones and vitriol, and to endure in silence the unmanly insults of the pro-slavery press. The simple and direct sincerity of her mind, her forgetfulness of self, and her tranquil courage, carried conviction to the minds of thousands that she had a message worth listening to. But at first many even of her own religious community thought it necessary to show their disapprobation of her conduct, by refusing to recognise her when they met. She owned that this "had caused her considerable pain," but it never caused her to swerve for a moment from the course she felt to be that of duty. She usually took a share of the seat behind the door in railway cars, because that place was ordinarily assigned to negroes, and would converse kindly with her fellow-passengers there.

At the celebrated trial in 1859 of Daniel Dangerfield, a fugitive slave, Lucretia Mott remained all through the long hours of suspense by the side of the prisoner. The trial and the courthouse were watched by two crowds, both in the greatest anxiety and suspense, one hoping for the release, the other, and by far the larger and more dangerous, hoping for the condemnation of the man. At last the long trial ended in victory for the right. Daniel Dangerfield was declared a free man; but the authorities of the court thought it would be impossible to get him away in safety through the angry pro-slavery crowd, without an escort of police. Their fears were found to be groundless, for when the doors of the court were thrown open, and the slave walked out, a free man, Lucretia Mott, the aged Quaker lady, was by his side; her hand on his arm was a sufficient protection, and he passed through the angry crowd in safety.

Very soon after this came the War of Secession. The Abolitionists knew, though the politicians did not, that this war would decide the question of slavery. As all the world knows now, they were right. The American people were enabled to prevent the secession of the slave states; and in 1863 a proclamation of President Lincoln announced the Abolition of Slavery in the United States. Lucretia Mott lived for seventeen years after this crowning victory of her life's labours. She died on 11th November 1880, universally respected, and loved by those who knew her.

Elizabeth Fry
Mary Carpenter
Caroline Herschel
Sarah Martin
Mary Somerville
Queen Victoria
Harriet Martineau
Florence Nightingale
Mary Lamb
Agnes Elizabeth Jones
Charlotte & Emily Brontë
Elizabeth Barrett Browning
Lady Sale and her fellow hostages
                    in Afghanistan
Elizabeth Gilbert
Jane Austen
Maria Edgeworth
Queen Louisa of Prussia
Dorothy Wordsworth
Sister Dora

MB Barbauld
Joanna Baillie
Hannah More
Prudence Crandall &
    Lucretia Mott

Term	Date	Talk
Spring 2008	08.01.08	The Oxford Dictionary of National Biography
	22.01.08	Women in the Air
	05.02.08	The Story of Chastleton House
	19.02.08	A Short History of Jazz, and some Major Players
	04.03.08	Village Life in Malta
	18.03.08	A.G.M. & Bring & Buy
	01.04.08	The Boxer Rebellion
	15.04.08	The Stone Walls of Headington Quarry
Summer 2008	06.05.08	Turning Life into Fiction
	20.05.08	Roald Dahl's War
	03.06.08	Members' Afternoon
	10.06.08	Excursion
	17.06.08	The History and Work of the Blue Cross
	01.07.08	The Development of the Printed Map in Oxfordshire
	15.07.08	Summer Party
Autumn 2008	16.09.08	Yukon - the last great Gold Rush
	07.10.08	The Green Gym
	21.10.08	Custer and the Little Bighorn
	04.11.08	Working Backstage
	18.11.08	Recent Discoveries in Oxford Castle
	09.12.08	Christmas Party

CPSIA information can be obtained at www.ICGtesting.com
Printed in the USA
BVOW04s1014070515

399428BV00013B/182/P